TOWN & VILLAGE DISCOVERY TRAILS

Cheshire

Abigail Bristow, Tom Hornby, Norman James and Les Lumsdon

SIGMA
Leisure

Published by Sigma Leisure – an imprint of
Sigma Press, 1 South Oak Lane, Wilmslow, Cheshire SK9 6AR, England.

British Library Cataloguing in Publication Data
A CIP record for this book is available from the British Library.

ISBN: 1 85058 485 0

Typesetting and Design by: Sigma Press, Wilmslow, Cheshire.

Cover Design: MFP Design & Print

Cover Photograph: Oak Cottages, Styal (Nick Lambert)

Printed by: MFP Design & Print

Preface

The authors of this book are all branch officers of the East Cheshire Transport 2000 Group. Transport 2000 is a campaigning group which aims to promote the provision of more environmentally friendly and sustainable transport systems. One way to bring about these objectives is to encourage travellers to use public transport for leisure pursuits, and it is for that reason that they have written this guide to discovering the town and village history and geography of Cheshire, providing a guide to thirty towns and villages throughout the county, nearly all of which are accessible by public transport, either local bus or train.

We hope that you will not only enjoy the town and village trails listed in this book, but that you will take the opportunity to try out the public transport system which can provide extra enjoyment on your day out. We realise, however, that it is not possible for everyone to use public transport at all times, and we have therefore provided detailed access descriptions for travel by car with recommended parking details for each trail. Please be considerate when parking, especially in the smaller villages, as your parking space is likely to be close to someone's dwelling place!

It has proved difficult to select just thirty walks, as Cheshire is a large county with a socially and geographically diverse range of towns and villages. However, we hope that we have been able to provide you with an insight into the fascinating urban and village life of Cheshire, and that you will be encouraged to continue your explorations independently.

Abigail Bristow, Tom Hornby, Norman James and Les Lumsdon

Contents

Location Map

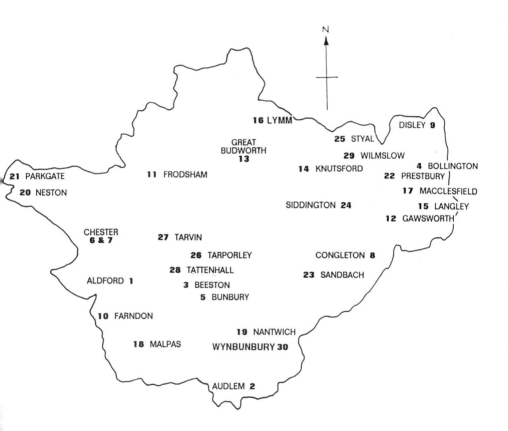

Introduction

Cheshire is perhaps best known for its gently undulating plain which rises up to the high hills of the Peak District. Herds of cows graze peacefully in the richest of meadows and sheep are fattened on the higher flanks to the east. It is very much a rural county where you find field after field of green pasture broken only by sandstone ridges and rivers of character such as the Dee and the Dane. There are also dozens of historic mansions surrounded by exquisite parklands, many of which have been created by the great landscape gardeners of the time. For Cheshire is where many early industrialists retired to from Manchester, having made their fortunes in textile production.

For many the joy of the county lies not only in the paths and bridleways which span the countryside but also in its villages and towns themselves. This book offers an introduction to many of these places – it is a starting point for exploration. Those who are deep into historical research may be disappointed, for this is not a historic treatise; the book is, however, packed with yarns and notes about important buildings to be seen and visited.

Cheshire certainly is a county of variety and its principal towns are very different in layout and character. Compare, for example, the market places of Audlem and Malpas in the south of the county, which clearly have been untouched by industrialisation, to those of Congleton and Macclesfield where textile production has shaped their existence during the past two centuries. The procurement of salt has also been an important factor in the development of several Cheshire towns. Nantwich was an extremely important salt town in earlier times and its magnificent array of half-timbered buildings makes it a must to visit. Northwich grew up as another important salt town and its history is told in the Salt Museum.

Several of Cheshire's fine market towns are included, each having its very own special feature. The crosses at Sandbach, set back in a cobbled square are one such sight, the landmark of White Nancy above Kerridge another, or the Buttermarket at Audlem. Each town tends to have a quarter where architectural standards have been retained and these are the places to stay awhile to absorb the atmosphere. When walking around it is as well to look up as often as possible for basic facades at street level often obscure handsome Georgian and Victorian buildings.

The real pleasure lies in imagining what life would have been like in previous centuries, and how the village or town has evolved in terms of both trade and social custom. There is often a mediaeval core which towns have outgrown. Macclesfield is a classic example. Walk up the 108 steps to the high point of a bluff above the River Bollin and you witness this core. Here is the ancient church of St Michael and the marketplace with a street layout which clearly dates from the earlier centuries. Beyond are the layers of development, the mills of the silk manufacturing era and then through to post-industrial retailing sprawl. We are fortunate that so much has survived; this book aims to bring to life these parts of our towns and villages which we tend to take for granted. The alleys and courtyards, the riverside paths, the open spaces given over to parkland, make up our urban heritage as much as the prominent buildings; they need to be cherished.

Chester

The county town, Chester, is widely acclaimed as a tourism destination. It draws visitors from throughout the world and at times appears to be overwhelmed by it all. At the height of the season it is hard to find room on the pavement. From Roman times, through to the last century, each successive generation has added architectural interest to the city. By far the most impressive legacies of the medieval period are The Rows – balconies above street level which offer shelter and security in shopping. The walls are magnificent too. They provide an inner sanctum. No longer are they defensive but they bring a tranquillity to several quarters. Coupled with the canals and the River Dee, they provide a network of traffic free paths which allow you the opportunity to visit almost every nook and cranny of the city. The two walks chosen for this book bring out the very best of Chester.

The villages, of course, are much quieter. Those included in the book are the larger communities rather than the hamlet with little more than a shop and village inn. Some have even lost these now. They include places such as Gawsworth with its exceptional Hall and Tarporley where Georgian buildings grace the main street and coaching inns stand almost in anticipation of a coaching revival. Styal is rather different; here is a village and mill built in early industrial times and doing its utmost to shut out the world of traffic and noise both from the roads and nearby Manchester Airport. Despite this intrusion the National Trust manages to provide a splendid village setting which is authenticity itself. You will not fail to be impressed if you have not been yet.

There are so many other locations that deserve to be included but had to be omitted because of constraints of space. Astbury with its very fine church, the hillside village of Rainow with its surviving horse trough and unusual allegorical Mellor Gardens, are but two which come readily to mind. Others such as Marbury, Peckforton, and Wildboarclough are equally deserving but perhaps the authors will be prompted in due course to write up a companion book.

Travel

It is no coincidence that most of the villages and towns chosen are well served by public transport. As a group of authors we are keen to encourage people to become less dependent on the car. In terms of the places you visit it will make far less impact in terms of congestion and parking. Why not try a journey by train or bus instead?

Most public transport services in the county are publicised in several timetable books which are available at Tourist Information Centres, libraries and bus stations. The booklets cover the following areas:

1. Warrington
2. Runcorn and Widnes
3. Ellesmere Port and Neston

4. Northwich and Winsford
5. Macclesfield
6. Chester
7. Crewe and Nantwich
8. Congleton
9. Local Rail Services

There is also a telephone information service available, as follows:

Warrington: 01925 444250

Wilmslow: 01625 534850

Crewe: 01270 505350

Chester: 01244 602666

Runcorn: 01928 704450

Northwich: 01606 815050

These are open Monday to Friday, 8am until 6pm, Saturday 9am until 1pm. A minicom facility is available.

Train Information

At the time of writing information is available by phoning 0345 484950.

The Strolls

The idea is to explore each village or town at your own pace, dwelling at key vantage points, calling in at attractions, stopping at cafes or pubs for light refreshments. Most of the strolls are between one and two miles and for the best part they include few hills so they are accessible to most people. We provide hints and guidance on walks and attractions further afield from the featured towns and villages to allow further exploration if you wish.

What to Wear

The walks are mainly on pavements, tracks and across a few fields only on link paths. Therefore, it is possible to enjoy these walks without boots or sturdy footwear. Trainers or light walking shoes will be fine in all but the wettest of circumstances. It is always sensible to take a waterproof jacket or umbrella should the weather change suddenly.

The invitation is before you. If you have a spare morning or afternoon take a look at someone else's town or village, learn a little more about Cheshire and most of all about conserving all that is best in our communities. You might join a local history society or Civic Society group if the interest really grows. However, we hope that you enjoy these 30 strolls in Cheshire. If you have a whole day, or a few days to spare, you can combine a number of the walks and make the most of the delightful county of Cheshire.

1. Aldford

Access

Aldford is a small village in west Cheshire, next to the B5130, five miles south of Chester. There is no off-street parking. It is recommended that you park in the village on School Lane at SJ419593.

Bus services run to and from Chester, Farndon and Wrexham. Alight at Aldford Bridge. Full details are obtainable from Cheshire Bus: phone numbers are listed in the introduction.

The old school, Aldford (Norman James)

The Village

Aldford is a particularly attractive village laid out in almost rectangular form. It was re-constructed as a designed village in the middle of the last century by Sir Richard Grosvenor, 2nd Marquis of Westminster because it was felt that something had to be done about the state of the parish church. This dated from the 14th century and had fallen into a very poor state of repair. Records show that boys from the village were being paid to rid it of sparrows, adders and hedgehogs which were wandering in through gaps in the structure.

In his wisdom, Sir Richard decided that the entire village should be rebuilt! The imposing new church dominates the village.

Refreshments

The village has one public house, the Grosvenor Arms, which serves food mid-day and evenings. There is also a Post Office and village store.

Nearby Places of Interest

Eaton Hall

Eaton Hall is immediately to the north of the village; set in extensive grounds which are opened to the public periodically. Several public footpaths lead through the estate.

Watling Street

Excavations about a mile south of Aldford have revealed a road surface and kerb stones which once formed part of the Roman Road known as Watling Street.

Farndon and Holt

Four miles to the south are the picturesque twin towns of Farndon and Holt; one in England and the other in Wales. They are on opposite banks of the Dee and are joined by an ancient bridge. (See Walk No. 10)

Bruera

Situated a little over a mile north east of Aldford, the pretty church in the tiny settlement of Bruera is well worth a visit.

The Walk

1. The walk starts from the church in Church Lane at SJ419594. Across the road is the Post Office and village store.

2. Explore the pleasant churchyard with views of the village and surrounding fields and woods. There is an ancient cross, restored in 1901.

The church, rebuilt of local sandstone in the mid-nineteenth century (but in late thirteenth century style) is very big considering the size of the village. Its most distinctive feature is the west tower with its coni-

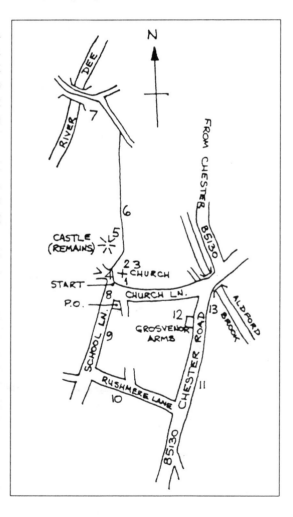

cal roofed SW stair turret. The wooden spire was added ten years after consecration.

Several features from earlier buildings were incorporated into the new church, such as many of the wall plaques and the ancient stone over the south doorway which came from the fourteenth century tower, in which it was inverted, indicating that it probably had already been used in an even earlier building.

3. In the old church, singing had been accompanied by stringed instruments. The new building was provided with an organ. This was originally in the west of the building but, in 1902, the blind organist dismantled it and then re-built it in its present position.

4. Leave the churchyard by crossing over the sandstone stile to the west of the church into the small lane beyond. Turn right and pass through the white gate ahead.

5. In front of you are the remains of the Motte and Bailey Castle which dates from about the mid twelfth century, when a Robert de Aldford is recorded as having lived here. The north aisle of the church was built over the ditch which surrounded the bailey. Behind you, in the north wall of the churchyard, note the odd arches to each side of the gate through which you have just passed.

6. The path here follows the 'Marches Way' and is clearly defined. Cross the first field diagonally to the right, to reach an old oak tree with exposed roots. The path then bears left-wards. The earthworks of the Motte and Bailey Castle are close by to your left. The way follows an almost straight line across fields to reach a small gate leading to a tarmaced drive. Turn left and follow the drive which continues through woodland a short distance before reaching the beautiful Iron Bridge spanning the River Dee.

7. The roadway across the bridge is a public footpath and offers splendid views along the tree lined river. The bridge is built near the site of the ford which carried the Roman road, Watling Street, across the Dee. When the Dee was low, the paved causeway of the ford, formed of large stones, is reported to have been visible in the river bed. The settlement at the ford became known by the Anglo Saxon name "The Old Ford," which is thought to have given rise to the modern name of Aldford.

8. Retrace your steps to the church. The view of the church as you approach across the fields is particularly impressive. Pass through the gate into the narrow lane beside the church and continue to Church Lane, with the church to your left. At the junction of Church Lane and School Lane, continue forward into School Lane.

9. School Lane was the site of the original village and lies on the alignment of Watling Street. You will notice that the lane is lined by sandstone walls topped with hedges, as are most of the lanes in the village. You will also see that almost every building has been constructed in a different style. The lovely school building on the right is now used by a firm of engineering consultants. The thatched cottage to be seen a little further along, also on your right, is the only building which survives from the old village of Aldford prior to the mid-nineteenth century reconstruction. Note its particularly tall chimneys.

10. Shortly, you will reach Rushmere Lane. The house on the left-hand corner has ornate painted plaster work. Turn left into Rushmere Lane. After a short distance, you will pass the end of Middle Lane and, continuing straight ahead, will enter Green Lake Lane. To the right, there are views over the surrounding fields, as there are no hedges at this point.

11. At the next junction you reach Chester Road, the B5130, not a very busy road. Here, turn left. Along here you will pass a succession of fascinating buildings. One of the first is the old school house, now a private home. Several old farm buildings further along are no longer required for agriculture and have been put to new uses, providing accommodation for several businesses. To your right, are fine views of fields and woods.

12. A little further on is The Grosvenor Arms; a most impressive public house, built in 1892 with many rooms and featuring walls lined with books. There is a garden with tables to the rear. This is a very pleasant spot in fine weather.

13. Just beyond the pub, on your right, are the village stocks, set into the sandstone wall. Continue a short distance and turn into Church Lane on your left, immediately before Aldford Bridge. Pass the gates of Eaton Hall. As you stroll along, you will pass beautiful brick built cottages to left and right, several with ornate twisted chimneys. The road takes you past the fine village hall and passes the end of Middle Lane to, once again, reach the church and the starting point of the walk.

2. Audlem

Access

The village of Audlem (SJ660436) lies in south Cheshire on the A529, five miles south of Nantwich. There is a car park to the north of the village, just off the A529 to the right on entering the village.

There are frequent bus services to and from Crewe and Nantwich; full service details can be obtained from Cheshire Busline: numbers are listed in the Introduction.

The Village

Audlem is a very pleasant canal-side village (some would describe it as a small town) dating from medieval times. The Shropshire Union Canal descends to the Cheshire Plain here through a series of fifteen locks: hard work for the boaters, but a splendid sight of a summer's afternoon. The village offers a series of charming vistas, and it can be very pleasant aimlessly wandering the streets, enjoying the scenes which open up and the historic buildings and the street life.

Refreshments

There are several fine pubs in Audlem, mentioned in the text, and also the Priest House Coffee Shop in Stafford Street.

Nearby Places of Interest

Daffields Craft Centre

Daffields Working Farm and Craft Centre lies 2.5 miles north of Audlem, and offers opportunities for an interesting excursion.

Hankelow

The village of Hankelow lies just to the north of Audlem, and is worth a visit to see the duck pond on the village green, which is fenced in to prevent the duck inhabitants from wandering off! But why would they want to wander off, when such attractive duck houses are provided?

Shropshire Union Canal

Towpaths lead alongside the Shropshire Union canal to the north and south of Audlem, offering pleasant, easy strolls and rambles.

The Buttermarket at Audlem (Norman James)

The Walk

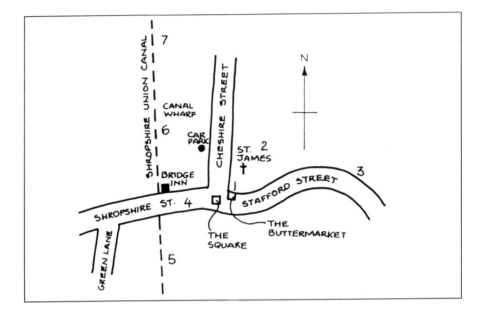

1. The trail starts at the village Buttermarket, outside the church of St James. The Buttermarket dates from 1773, and was restored in 1992. This fine structure housed a weekly butter market until 1914. Take a look here at the bear stone hewn out of Cumberland granite; the iron ring allowed bears to be tethered and baited here. The original location of the bear stone was in the middle of the square. In the middle of the square today stands a memorial and lamp standard in memory of Richard Baker Bellyse.He was a surgeon in Audlem for 40 years, who died in 1877. Walk slightly north along Cheshire Street to see the Village Hall to the left, and the Lamb public house to your right.

2. Now make your way back to the church of St James the Great, built from red Cheshire sandstone. The clock was installed in 1911 at the Coronation of George V and Queen Mary. The ancient mass dial stone is well worth viewing; it dates from Saxon times, and was moved to its present position in the 16th century, when it was also unfortunately mounted upside down. It was used to

tell when the church masses were due. There is some particularly fine old stained glass in the church windows. The views from this pleasant churchyard open up pleasingly in most directions from a variety of angles. Take some time to wander awhile here.

3. From the church, turn left down Stafford Street, passing the Old Priest House Coffee Shop to your right, open for fine food and provisions 09.00 to 17.00 daily. Further along Stafford Street you will find the Village Post Office, and some attractive dwelling houses converted from what were formerly village shops. Now make your way back to the Square and continue onwards, westwards, along Shropshire Street.

4. You will pass the Co-operative building to your left, and then a shop which fulfils the dual function of newsagents and drapers. Further along Shropshire Street on your left you will find Audlem Methodist church and an attractive drinking fountain. To your right you will pass successively, the Lord Combermere public house, the village fire station, and a shop selling antiques and fishing tackle; another example of the ingenuity of Audlem shopkeepers.

5. On reaching the Bridge Inn, turn left (south) along the Shropshire Union canal towpath, from where you will be able to enjoy fine views over the south Cheshire countryside. You will be able to pass the series of canal locks for about a mile. Take note that the towpath here can be muddy in wet weather. When you are in need of refreshment, make you way back to the Bridge Inn, originally built as a canal tavern for the benefit of bargees in the 1830s. It originally also had stabling for the bargees' horses.

6. Continue northwards from the Bridge Inn along the canal wharf; you will find steps to the left leading down to the canal towpath. You will find several interesting buildings here on the wharf, including the Shroppie Fly public house, converted from a warehouse in the 1970s, and also Audlem Mill Canal Shop and Workshop, built in 1916 and originally oil-powered; it continued to mill grain and produce animal feedstuffs until 1970. There is a very attractive lock-keeper's cottage, and beyond that a marina;

note that many of the boat moorings here are permanent and that there are gardens adjacent to many of the canal boats. This is lock 13 out of 15 in this sequence, which raises boats to and from the Cheshire plain.

7. Continue to walk along the canal towpath until you reach the bottom lock by the bridge. You will be able to enjoy fine views in all directions here, and particularly to your right where you will able to see the very beautiful Moss Hall, an Elizabethan timber-framed hall dating from the 1600s which had its own ghost and was rumoured to have its own subterranean passage to the village church. There is also a fine flock of swans which tend to frequent the canal at this point. When you have walked far enough along the canal, make your way back to the centre of the village and avail yourself of the services offered by the fine public houses, hotels, and coffee shop.

3. Beeston & Peckforton

Access

Beeston lies one mile west of the A49, north of Whitchurch, east of Chester.

The Village

The village of Beeston (SJ542586) is small and attractive, but the main attractions of this walk are the opposing castles of Beeston and Peckforton. A rival attraction is the Pheasant at Higher Burwardsley.

Refreshments

Refreshments can be obtained within Peckforton Castle grounds, and at the Pheasant public house at Higher Burwardsley.

The Walk

1. Beeston Castle has a large car park directly opposite the main entrance, which is free to visitors. Beeston Castle is operated by English Heritage; there is an admission charge, with discounts for children and pensioners. The castle, dating from the 13th century, built by Sir Ranulph de Blundeville and inspired by what he had seen during his travels abroad, including the crusades. There is a small museum by the entrance gate. The walk to the castle takes you along a well trodden path, up an attractive hillside. The remains of the castle are reached by crossing a new,

Medieval pursuits at Peckforton Castle (Abigail Bristow)

though elegant and steep, bridge. The views are stunning in all directions, though perhaps especially across to the next hill, topped by Peckforton Castle. Beeston Castle itself affords plenty of scope for a lengthy visit, with space for picnics on the hillside. Toilets are available, near the entrance gate.

2. On leaving Beeston Castle, the choice is to drive to Peckforton Castle or to walk through the attractive village of Beeston. Whatever your choice the route is the same: turn left out of the car park and follow the narrow lane into Beeston. Turn left out of this lane, then turn right past a curious house with an inset post-box. The road is a quiet country lane, the few houses have very tall and

intricate chimneys. The
road bears left, there are
open fields to one side
and woodland to the
right.

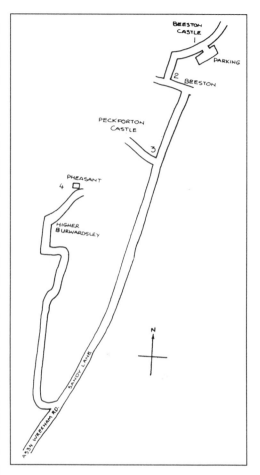

3. The entrance to Peckforton Castle is to the right,
a winding lane takes you
through woodland and
up to the castle and sur-
rounding parking space.
Peckforton Castle is a
complete contrast to the
authentic ruin of Beeston
Castle. Peckforton was
built in the mid nine-
teenth century by John,
later Lord Tollemache,
the local member of par-
liament. The castle is an
impressive replica of a
medieval construction.
As it is in one piece and
real medieval castles tend
not to be, it is also in demand as a film location
and has hosted Robin
Hood and Sherlock Holmes.

The castle also has an attractive cafe and grounds which on
occasion host costumed fights. There is an admission charge.

4. The next step is either the walk back to Beeston Castle or a drive
to the Pheasant at Higher Burwardsley (SJ522565). This pub is
quite difficult to find, follow the road map carefully, but, well
worth the trouble. There is a very cute green parrot in the bar,
and food in the restaurant. The beer is excellent.

4. Bollington and Kerridge

Access

Bollington (SJ935785) enjoys a good daily bus service from Macclesfield, and a lesser direct service from Stockport. Get off at the Waggon and Horses for Adlephi Mill. If travelling by car you should travel on the B5091 from the Macclesfield by-pass road. There is parking near to Adelphi Mill.

Macclesfield Canal, Bollington (Norman James)

The Village

Bollington is a large village, some would say a small township, which lies three miles north of Macclesfield. It nestles in the narrow Dean valley beneath the ridge of Kerridge. Affectionately called 'Happy Valley', Bollington owes much of its heritage to the industrial revolution, when at the height of its prosperity, in the mid-nineteenth century, there were some 13 mills providing work in the thriving cotton industry. Though the production of cotton, and later synthetic fibres, has all but ceased now, two of the most magnificent examples, Adelphi (1856) and Clarence mills (1841 but dating from much earlier), are again enjoying renewed life as offices, restaurants, shops and workshops.

The main street, known as Henshall Rd, Wellington Rd and Palmerston Street, runs up the valley from Bollington Cross to the Turners Arms, where the road for Pott Shrigley parts company with the road into Ingersley Vale Road and Church Street. From this main artery, streets peel off to different parts of the village, Grimshaw Lane leading up to Kerridge from the Waggon and Horses, and the Adlington Road to the Recreational Ground, for example. There are a few shops on the High Street; but they are nearly outnumbered by public houses, many of which were built to serve the thirsty workforce from the mills. Wherever you walk in Bollington, it is not far from a place of refreshment!

Neighbouring Kerridge is on higher ground than Bollington, a smaller and quieter settlement which grew up primarily to house workers in nearby quarries, which are still working. Dressed stone from Kerridge saddle is in keen demand for roofs, walls and paving stones by those who seek to build dwellings in traditional style. In the last century much of the stone was shipped out by boat on the Macclesfield Canal and the waggonway is a feature of this walk.

Refreshments

Many pubs in the area offer lunches and early evening meals. Several also cater well for families, such as the Cock and Pheasant at

Bollington Cross. There are also restaurants and a cafe in the Palmerston Street area through which you pass.

Nearby Places of Interest

White Nancy

This curious monument perched on the northern tip of Kerridge Ridge was built by the Gaskell family in the early years of the 19th century to commemorate the Battle of Waterloo. It has since been a place where beacons are lit to celebrate major events. Much loved by the people of the area, the folly has weathered well despite the occasional spot of vandalism.

Rainow

While in the area, visit the nearby village of Rainow where there were nine mills situated near to the River Dean in the late 18th century and early 19th century. The older part of the village stands around the church on the main road. You will find several old lanes leading into the countryside and near to the Robin Hood pub is a set of village stocks – not used in recent times! An authentic horse trough stands to the west of the village centre.

The Walk

1. Start the walk from the Adelphi Mill car park in Grimshaw Lane. Below the entrance is the Middlewood Way, at one time the Macclesfield, Bollington and Marple Railway which was opened formally in 1869.

2. From the car park, between the first two buildings, climb up steps to the Macclesfield Canal, which was opened in the 1830s, a fairly late arrival in the canal era. This was one of the prettiest canals, virtually following a 500 ft contour and winding its way through East Cheshire to Kidsgrove, where it unceremoniously joins the Trent and Mersey trunk canal. The roving bridges (which enabled

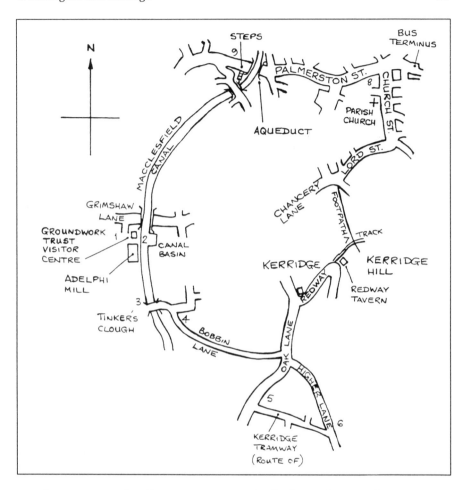

horses to and milestones are particularly endearing features. Go right to pass Adelphi Mill, built by the Swindells family as a steam driven cotton factory and remaining as a textile producer until the late 1960s.

3. Leave the canal at the first bridge, up steps on the right and then left over the bridge itself. On your right is Tinker's Clough which is where the canal burst its banks in the early hours of the morning on February 29, 1912. There was no loss of life but considerable damage. It is said that local people waded through the gushing waters to catch the fish for supper.

4. Keep ahead on the unmade track, known as Bobbin Lane, which looks rural but was, as its name suggests, where several of the buildings, such as Bobbin Cottage, were bobbin producers. Here was also Beehive Mill, of which only a pair of gates remains. You pass by them. To your left you will see across fields the Lukic-Belgrade Hotel. This used to be Hollin Hall, the home of the Davenport Family, in the last century.

5. You reach Oak Lane. Go right and at the next junction with a crossroads of tracks, go left through a gateway. This is the Kerridge Tramway, built to link Endon Quarries with a wharf on the canal. The gradient gets steeper as you walk up to Endon Cottage. Here the incline would have run beneath the Victoria Bridge behind the cottage. Steam power would almost certainly have been used on this section and horses on the lower run.

6. Before Endon Cottage at the junction, go left to follow Higher Lane by delightful stone cottages back into the centre of Kerridge. Go right at the junction and walk up to the junction of Jackson Lane and Redway. Go right up to the Redway Tavern. Go left into the car park but then turn right up a track which runs up to a field beneath White Nancy.

7. Once through the gateway and over the cattle-grid go left down the field on a slab path. This brings you down to a stile and onto Lord Street. Go downhill and by the bleachworks. Keep left to pass Bollington church and the Church Inn to Palmerston Street.

8. Go left here to wander down through the heart of the village where butcher and baker survive with traditional pubs such as the Meridian and Spinners Arms. You pass the shell of the old church on the right and the road bends to traffic lights and under the viaduct, something of a masterpiece and evidently engineered by a colleague of Thomas Telford, Charles Nichol.

9. Take care to cross the road to the steps set back in the wall. They lead up to the canal towpath and are steep. Once on the towpath go right to return to Adelphi Mill.

5. Bunbury

Access

The village of Bunbury (SJ569581) lies in south Cheshire, half a mile west of the A41, approximately one mile south east of the A51. There is limited on-street parking on the main road around Bunbury locks, and also around the village green in Higher Bunbury in front of the church.

Bus services to Bunbury run principally to and from Chester, Nantwich and Crewe. Full service details are available from the Cheshire Busline: see the telephone numbers listed in the Introduction.

The Dysart Arms, from the churchyard (Norman James)

The Village

Bunbury is an attractive medieval village graciously nestling around its fine church dedicated to St Boniface. It is possible to enjoy many a fine walk through this attractive village, enjoying the fine flowers in the public gardens, and the street views along the narrow winding lanes. Bunbury lies on the Shropshire Union Canal, and the pleasant Bunbury locks, some one mile north of the main village, also offer pleasant walking opportunities along the canal towpaths. Bunbury also boasts a splendid water mill, now lovingly restored and open to the public, following its destruction in 1968.

Refreshments

The Dysart Arms, opposite the church of St Boniface, offers an ideal opportunity to eat and drink in pleasant surroundings. Alternative pubs are situated in the lower village: the Nags Head and the Crewe Arms.

Nearby Places of Interest

Shropshire Union Canal

As outlined above, there are very pleasant walks along the banks of the Shropshire Union Canal; a chandlery at the Bunbury Locks wharf sells a good range of guide books and memorabilia concerned with this stretch of inland water, and with canals in general.

Beeston Castle

Beeston Castle lies only two miles away, and offers an attractive option for a longer excursion from Bunbury.

Footpaths

There are many footpaths leading from Bunbury in most directions, which can be followed with the aid of an Ordnance Survey map. Particularly worthy of note are the paths to Beeston and Haughton Moss.

The Walk

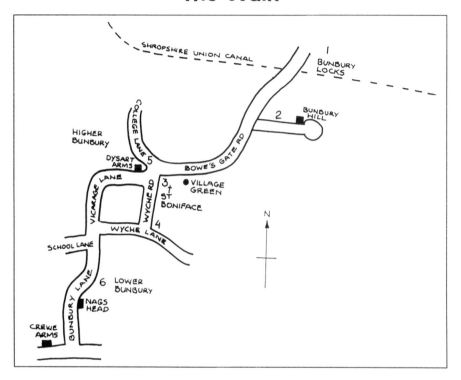

1. The walk starts at Bunbury Locks, one mile north of the village centre on the Shropshire Union Canal (SK578591). This fine working wharf features some high rise locks, and a useful chandlery where you can stock up on canal provisions or guides. Note also the fine canal horse stables to the east of the wharf. Walk south towards the village centre along the pleasant meandering country lane, passing beautiful county houses and ·slowly-flowing streams.

2. After some half a mile you will come to a left turning, signposted to Bunbury Mill. A 200 yard walk along this road brings you to this fine building, for which there are guided tours, although the opening times may be limited. A mill has stood on this site for some 700 years; This one dates from the 1840s, but was destroyed in 1968, before being lovingly restored between 1974-7.

3. Retrace your way to the main road, and walk a further half a mile to the village centre. You will come across the attractive sight of the church of St Boniface, towering splendidly above the village green and the surrounding houses, with the fine Dysart Arms public house to be glanced behind the church. This church has a particularly fine interior including sandstone columns. There are several interesting artefacts to be viewed within including the figures made by itinerant journeymen on their way to Vale Royal Abbey in 1450. The tomb of Sir Hugh de Calveley can also be viewed; this structure stands some two metres tall: Sir Hugh founded Bunbury's collegiate church and was reputed to be a giant, some seven feet tall.

4. Emerging from the splendid churchyard, turn left in front of the Dysart Arms and wander along Wyche Road. Along this lane you will encounter the beautiful Chantry House, be able to glimpse an attractive private pond, and also take the opportunity to wander Bunbury's by-ways to admire the houses, gardens and street scenes.

5. Return to the church and pass beyond it to take a close look at the alms houses, dating from 1874. Make your way back to the Dysart Arms; now it is time to enjoy the splendours of this lovely county pub, built some 200 years ago and originally part of the Tollemache estate. It boasts a comfortable bar, a pleasant lounge with beams and a fire; and also, a wonderful large garden where you can sup your pint, and enjoy your food, while overlooking the splendours of the marvellous church of St Boniface.

6. There is also a lower village to Bunbury; from the Dysart Arms turn right and bear right-wards along Vicarage Lane, which will bring you eventually to the lower village. This is a delightful walk passing several fine thatched buildings, offering fine views of the countryside, and passing by the Nags Head public house in the lower village. If you continue to the junction with the main road you will come across the Crewe Arms. Now retrace your steps to the upper village and the start of the walk.

6. Chester:
The Cathedral Walk

Access

It is recommended that cars are left in one of the three 'park and ride' car parks situated on the outskirts of the city. Frequent buses will take you to the city centre.

Chester is well served by train from many points in the North West as well as from London. National Express coaches also serve the city. There is a good network of local bus services. Frequent buses run between the railway station and the city centre. Details are available from Cheshire Bus: phone numbers listed in the introduction.

The City

The name Chester comes from the Roman word *Castra* meaning a camp, named after the important Roman fortress on the site. This was abandoned when the Romans left, but was restored in the 10th century by Ethelfleda of Mercia to defend the area from the Vikings.

The Roman Town Walls were extensively rebuilt in the Mediaeval period, and converted during the nineteenth century to a fashionable promenade.

A Minster seems already to have existed on the site of the present Cathedral before the Norman conquest. After the conquest, a Benedictine Abbey was built near the Minster and then, in the twelfth century, the reconstruction of the old Minster as a great Norman church was begun. After the Restoration, the disestablished Abbey was returned by Henry VII to be the new Anglican Cathedral building.

Chester was a stop on the first coach route known to run to a timetable. This was started in 1637 and ran between Birmingham and Holywell. A service from London was started in 1657. The journey took four days. This route, which was extended to Holyhead, became the route of the first mail coach, started in 1757. Later these services were replaced by the London to Holyhead railway which opened in 1850.

From the 1870s tourism began to emerge as a principal industry, the older linen and gloving industries being in decline. Chester now has a busy town centre which provides magnificent shopping facilities for the resident and visitor.

Refreshments

There are numerous pubs, restaurants and cafes in the city centre to suit all tastes. You will pass several on the walk.

The Walk

1. The walk starts from the Anglican Cathedral which is entered from St Warburgh Street at SJ404664, named after the Saint whose bones were said to lie in the old Minster. The Minster is well worth an hour's dalliance. The stained glass windows are particularly beautiful, especially the lovely blue of the Carter Shapland west window when it catches the afternoon sun. There is an exhibition area and gift shop.

2. St Warburgh Street houses shops and many fine old timber frame buildings. As you leave the Cathedral grounds, notice the stone building twenty yards to your right, now a shop but originally the mediaeval St Nicholas's Chapel. This building was later a Market Hall, but in 1777 it was licensed as a theatre and its distinguished performers included Charles Dickens in 1855.

3. Turn left into Bell Tower Walk, pleasantly shaded by trees overhanging from the Cathedral grounds. The modern Addleshaw Bell Tower in front of you is a startling contrast to the Cathedral. It was completed in 1975, the first free-standing bell

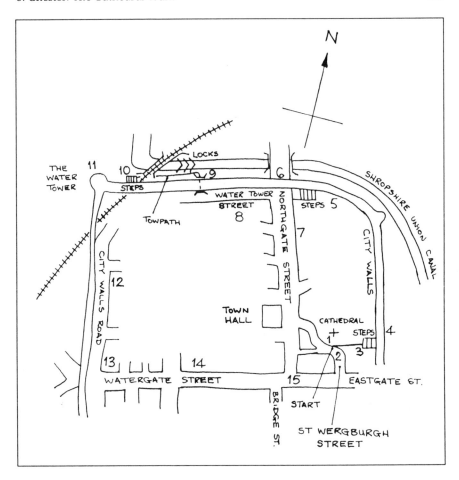

tower to be built in this country since the fifteenth century. From it, the congregation is summoned to services in the Cathedral. Here are seats on which to rest and admire the view.

4.   Mount the steps ahead of you to the old city walls and turn left. Continue along the walls, passing the Cathedral, and then playing fields, to your left. Shortly you will reach King Charles's Tower, from which Charles I watched his defeated army return to Chester in September 1645, four months before the surrender of the city to the Parliamentarian forces. Below you to your right is the Shropshire Union Canal, which also provides a pleasant traffic-free route across the city.

5.   The walls now turn to the left to reach Rufus Court on the left, housing several interesting shops, a restaurant a Jazz Theatre Bar and a tea-room. Next you reach the bridge over Northgate Street. This was the site of an important Roman Fortress, and later of the Mediaeval Gate which also housed the City Gaol. The present bridge was presented to the city in 1810 by the Earl of Grosvenor.

6.   After crossing Northgate Street by the bridge, take the steps to the left down to Water Tower Street. Return to Northgate Street and pass under the bridge. A spot just a little further down this busy road affords a striking view along the Canal, through a deep sandstone cutting, to the Welsh hill known as Moel Famau. Note the flying buttress supporting the stone walls to both sides.

7.   At this point, those more interested in the city centre shopping area can return directly along Northgate Street, past the impressive Town Hall, opposite which they can return to St Werburgh Street and the Minster.

8.   Those who wish to continue should return the short distance to Water Tower Street and make their way along it beside the wall. The old and new architectural styles on the left make a pleasing contrast. Notice the pretty nineteenth century terrace of Canning Street and the ornate, patterned gables of Edlingham Buildings dating from 1882. Opposite Pemberton Road, take the right turn under an arch through the city wall.

9.   Follow the cobbled pathway, which turns left and descends to the Shropshire Union Canal. Pass under the bridge carrying the main road. Note the monument, '1772 – 1972', commemorating the opening of the canal. Here is a spectacular flight of three locks. Note the special operating instructions for this complicated, though not unique, lock system. Descend alongside the canal. To your left, opposite the bottom lock, is a picnic area.

10.   After passing under the bridge carrying the Chester to Holyhead Railway over the Canal, bear left off the Towpath. Ahead and slightly to your left you will see stone steps leading up onto the wall. Straight ahead steps lead down to a recreation area with bowling and putting greens and tennis courts for the more sporting. You may wish to explore these before returning to the wall.

11. Re-joining the wall, proceed to the right to the Water Tower, so called because, when first built, it stood in the River Dee, which flowed below the wall at this point. The towers here acted as controls on shipping using this important waterway. Later, the river retreated and then silted to the point where it was not navigable by larger vessels. Today, the Dee is no longer even visible from the wall.

12. At the tower the wall turns left. The way leads down to City Walls Road. To your left is the Infirmary, built in 1761. Continue to the Bridge over Watergate Street, stopping to examine the – now, alas, defunct – marble drinking fountain set into the stonework of the bridge and dated 1857. Before the retreat of the Dee, all goods entering the city from the Port had to use this gate.

13. Turn left into Watergate Street, taking care as you cross City Walls Road as vehicles hurtle heedlessly under the bridge with a poor view. Admire the elegant, eighteenth century buildings as you progress up the street. There are also many earlier timber framed buildings. Cross St Martin's way, noting the old customs house building on the corner to the left and the adjacent Guild Hall, formerly the Church of the Holy Trinity.

14. Now entering the shopping area, look across to the right-hand side of the street to a fine timber framed building with carvings of scenes such as Adam and Eve and the Serpent. Cross the street to this building and mount the steps to the raised shopping gallery. These galleries, which house many interesting shops, as well as several pubs, are the famous Rows.

15. Continue across the end of Bridge Street into Eastgate Street. Ahead of you, on the bridge, is the ornate clock, dated 1897. Just before the bridge, turn right into a narrow alleyway from which steps lead up to the walls. Turn left, to cross the bridge. Continue the short distance back to the Minster and the start of the walk.

7. Chester: The River Walk

Access

Details of access can be found under 'Chester, The Cathedral Walk'.

The City

The city of Chester was first called Caer Leon by the pre-Roman inhabitants. It then became *Castra Deva*, a major Roman Fortress from before 74 AD, and was used in the assault on the Welsh tribes. It remained the control site at the northern end of the Welsh border and the lowest bridging point of the River Dee, until the early Middle Ages, as well as having the best port facilities north of Bristol.

Rome withdrew from Britain in 410 AD, and Chester's walls fell into disrepair until they were restored by the Mercians against the Vikings. Chester was subdued by the Normans in 1070 and passed to a succession of Norman Earls, and then to members of the Royal Family, whose duty it was until 1536 to hold the border against the Welsh.

As the River Dee silted, the Port was moved further and further downstream and the economic importance of Chester steadily reduced, but it is unrivalled for its architectural heritage and is an important shopping and tourist centre.

**The Eastgate Clock
(by permission, Chester City Council)**

Refreshments

The City centre has many pubs, cafes and restaurants, several of which are passed on the walk. There are similar facilities on the riverside promenade known as The Groves.

The Walk

The walk starts from Eastgate, famous for the clock which was erected in 1897 on a bridge which carries the city wall over Eastgate Street. Just to the west of the bridge, a little alley leads to steps taking you onto the wall.

2.   Turn right along the wall and go to Newgate, passing the watchtower base on the left. From Newgate bridge you can see the remains of the Roman amphitheatre. After crossing the bridge take the steps down to Park St. Turn right under the wall to Little St John's Street. The remains of the old mediaeval gate can be seen in the gardens to the right. Across the road to the left are the foundations of the south-east angle of the Roman fortress wall and internal tower. So, at this point, all the periods of town wall construction can be compared.

3.   Continuing along Little St John's Street, cross the end of Souters Lane to reach the Roman amphitheatre where crowds in Roman times, perhaps as many as 8,000 strong, came to witness the savage spectacles staged for their benefit. This, the largest Roman amphitheatre found in Britain, had walls over 30ft high. Walk across, or around, the ancient remains towards the Chester Visi-

tor Centre. Note the ornate frontage of Lumley Place across the
road to your left.

4. On rejoining Little St John's Street, take the narrow lane to the
right and pass the Parish Church of St John the Baptist. The
grounds of this church are well worth exploring, for the old

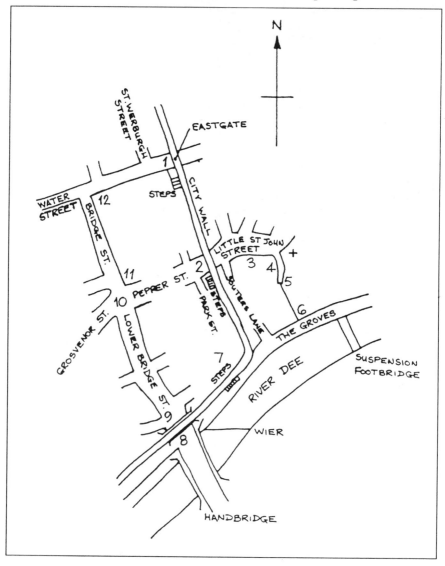

stonework seen to each end is the remains of the pre-Restoration Cathedral. Access can be gained through the iron gate to be found on your left, immediately after passing the church. Notice also the old tombstones used as flags. From the railings bounding the lower edge of the grounds is a fine view, through trees, of the Queen's Park suspension footbridge, rebuilt in 1923. Directly below can be seen The Hermitage, said to have been an anchorite's cell.

5. Return to the lane and, following the signpost for the River Dee, continue down the cobbled and paved path. A clearer view of The Hermitage can be seen to your left from the steps near the bottom of the path.

6. At the bottom, you reach The Groves, a pleasant riverside walk lined with trees. Here turn right. Along the riverside can be found refreshments of various types, places to sit, boats for hire and guided boat trips on the Dee. On the river can be seen a variety of water birds, including swans, which have returned after several years absence. Continuing, pass the end of Souters Lane. Here will be found a stop from which Chester Bus Tours run a frequent service of guided tours of the city. Proceeding, the City wall soon rejoins us from the right.

7. Ascend to the wall up the Recorders Step's, built for the convenience of Roger Comberbach, Recorder in 1700. Hotels and restaurants can be found along this stretch of the wall. In the river can be seen the weir which was built in the 11th. century to power a corn mill. Soon you reach the Old Dee Bridge built in 1387 to replace an older timber bridge which had been swept away by floods. This bridge, widened in 1826, was the lowest bridge across the River Dee until the 18th century. The suburb of Handbridge is visible across the river and was known in Welsh as Trebroeth, or "Burnt Town," as it was burnt frequently by the Welsh.

8. Cross the bridge over Lower Bridge Street, admiring the front of the unusually named Bear & Billet, originally built in 1664 as the town house of the Earl of Shrewsbury. Note Chester Hydro-Elec-

tric Power Station on the left immediately after the Old Dee Bridge. The Power Station was built in 1913 on the site of the old Dee corn mills.

9. Here, descend to Castle Drive. Turn left and go under the bridge left into Lower Bridge Street. Here buildings of many periods are to be seen. On your left you will reach the Old Kings Head, built in 1622 and remarkably well preserved. Cross over Lower Bridge Street to examine the building on the corner of the old, cobbled St Olaves Street opposite, where the structure of the timber frame – its windows appearing randomly placed – is evident. St Olaves church, really a chapel, is partly mediaeval but was restored in 1895. Further up Lower Bridge Street, on the left, is one of the oldest buildings, dated 1503.

10. Continuing, cross Pepper Street. A diversion left down Grosvenor Street will take you to the Grosvenor Museum which houses important Roman collections, and, further on, to the castle.

11. The Old St Michael's church on the corner of Bridge Street and Pepper Street now accommodates the Chester Heritage Centre. It stands on the site of the southern gateway of the Roman fortress. Ahead is Bridge Street, famous for its raised shopping galleries, known as The Rows. It is necessary to walk up and down the street on both sides to fully appreciate the many interesting features to be seen. For example, on the left are the 'Three Old Arches' which date from 1274. In addition to shops, there are also pubs, restaurants and fast food enterprises.

12. At the top of Bridge Street, with St Peter's church ahead, turn right into Eastgate Street. Here the Rows continue on the right of the street. A short stroll along Eastgate Street, with its many fine buildings, will return you to the start of the walk.

8. Congleton

Access

Congleton (SJ860630) is in the east of the county on the banks of the River Dane. It is very much an old silk town although very little textile production remains now. There are car parks in the central area of the town but Congleton is congested at the best of times.

The trail begins at the Fairground where all buses call. There is an hourly daily service (including Sundays) from Macclesfield and Crewe. Links to other places in Cheshire are thin on the ground. The railway station which is served by trains from Manchester and Stoke-on-Trent is well out of town and there is a good half mile walk along the A527 to the centre.

The Town

Congleton

The town's silk heritage is often overlooked in comparison to Macclesfield but Congleton was very important as a producer of textiles. It is thought that Congleton was a minor Roman settlement, most probably a crossing point of the Dane. There is certainly substantial evidence to suggest that Congleton grew up as a market centre in medieval times and in 1272 received a charter to hold fairs and markets on a weekly basis. Evidently, the township enjoyed a visit from King Edward I six years later and he granted permission to build a mill. During times of prosperity the lace and leather glove production thrived here. Much of this cottage industry was damaged in the 17th century when two plague epidemics hit the town with severity.

The Town Hall, Congleton
(Chris Rushton)

Scant evidence of these times survive, except for the Swan and Lion, which most probably dates from the 15th century, and the Bear's Head Hotel.

The shape of the town seen today stems from industrial times when silk mills flourished on the banks of the Dane. A number survive as some form of manufacturers of textiles, some in semi-dereliction and others enjoying re-use. There are pockets of handsome Georgian town houses and several quieter quarters which retain an air of Victorian pride, especially the Town Hall. Elsewhere traffic systems have made present day Congleton less than attractive and there are still jams which frustrate local people.

Refreshments

There are several cafes around the central shopping area as well as public houses throughout the town.

Nearby Places of Interest

Astbury

This is a very appealing settlement a little to the south of Congleton which decidedly merits a visit when in the area. The beautiful little village green leads to a church of considerable proportion. Enter by way of a solid stone gateway to the slightly elevated ground and admire the very fine Perpendicular architecture. There are effigies and tombs inside as well as exceptional woodwork from late medieval times. In the village you will find half-timbered houses, attractive brick cottages and a tea room. Nearby is a garden centre and a lake where there are walks as well as water sports.

Biddulph Valley Way

The Biddulph Valley way utilises the old railway track-bed of a line which ran through to the Potteries. It is popular with walkers and cyclists and offers a good introduction to the area, especially as you can use it to walk up to Biddulph Grange Gardens (National Trust).

Timbersbrook

No more than four or five miles from Congleton is the hamlet of Timbersbrook which grew up around a mill on a stream. From here you can walk up from the picnic site to Bosley Cloud (National Trust).

The Walk

1. Go left out of the Fairground, with your back to the library. At the corner of Market Street, go left again into High Street. By far the most impressive building here is the Town Hall, an ostentatious mock Gothic building.

2. Chapel Street leads off to the right, at one time called Back Lane and certainly an area known for cockfighting and bear baiting. Hence the famous tale of the civic gents spending the money saved for a bible on the purchase of a bear. On hearing from the

bear warden that the resident bear had expired just before the annual big fair the hard-up officials made this hasty decision! As you progress along Lawton Street several of the dwellings illustrate the wealth that was at one time available to build such town houses. Many of these remain and have steps up from pavement level. Nearby stood the great half-timbered house of John Bradshaw which was demolished in 1820. He was a staunch supporter of Cromwell and prepared the legal case against King Charles. He was the inventor of the bullet-proof hat!

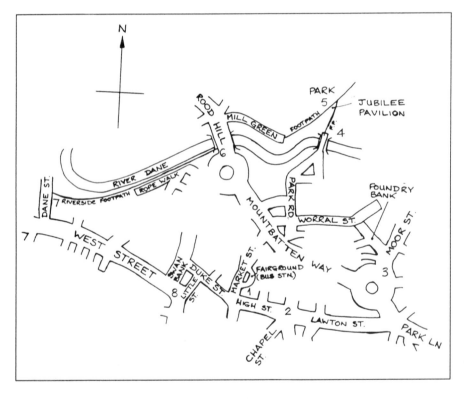

3. Cross Mountbatten Way and walk along Moor Street (A54). Leave the main road by the Dried Flower Factory Shop to walk down Foundry Bank. On the right stands Victoria Mill and below Shepherds Mill. Go left before the leisure centre into Worrall Street and then right into Park Road in an area known for its old mills, particularly the King's Mill, of which the first was built in the 15th century. To your left you will catch a glimpse of Riverside which has been restored in recent years and is now used as offices.

4. Cross the bridge over the Dane to Congleton Park. There is a weir to the left and in the park several unusual monuments, including a pillar and ancient cross, so take a wander to your right through the park which is in a lovely setting beneath Park Wood. The cross stood at one time opposite the Town Hall where you might expect to find it. It was in the last decade of the 19th century that the people of Congleton decided that it should be restored and re sited here and so it was duly erected in time for Coronation Day, i.e. the coronation of Edward VII in 1902. There is also a Victorian bandstand and water fountain in the park which also originates from this time.

5. Pass by and turn left by the Jubilee Pavilion, a building dating from 1887 which sadly has seen better times. As you leave the park you will see the small aviary on the right and greenhouses to the left. The path exits into the yard of R.H. Lowe. If you look to the left, you will see some ornate architecture but for the best part the mill is very functional. The road leads to a main road by the bridge over the River Dane at Rood Hill. To your right is the impressive structure of Salford Mill.

6. Cross the road and the bridge which dates from 1889, but pause if traffic permits, for from this height you can see what a haven for wildlife the river is in the town. What you see upstream is a re-modelled route following a devastating flood in 1451. Go right down a path which squeezes between a mill and the river to emerge near Rope walk (where rope was manufactured at one time). The path continues ahead but then rises away from the banks and to a set of steps out of the valley into Dane Street. Go left up to the Farmers Arms.

7. Turn left and walk by the handsome Georgian House, best admired through the wrought iron gates. Look down West Street and you will witness a range of good looking town houses including Milford House on the right and the Lion and Swan Inn.

There are many fascinating little architectural features here, for example, the tiling on the building opposite the inn.

8. Cross the road to walk down Little Street, which is medieval in layout if nothing else, into the pedestrian precinct. Look left to view the ornate Victorian buildings in Swan Bank. Most buildings in the precinct now illustrate modern facades but the narrow passages and upper storeys tell a story of earlier times where there would have been stables and workshops. At Market Street turn left to return to the Fairground. During the centuries this is where markets were held and nearby there would have been a busy industrial quarter. Things are different now.

9. Disley

Access

D isley is very accessible by public transport, having both a regular bus and train service from Manchester and Stockport. There is a very limited direct bus service from Macclesfield although it is possible to travel via Whaley Bridge, where you would change buses.

The A6 runs through Disley, a very busy road, which local residents resent. There is a car park near to the railway station.

The Village

This little village, lying in the Goyt Valley, is a little divorced from the rest of the county both geographically, and in that most people work in Greater Manchester. Nevertheless, the county is fortunate in retaining this settlement which is clustered around the cross-roads at Fountain Square. Here stands an impressive inn, which when stripped of commercial decoration is a fine building formerly a lodge to the Lyme estate. It was the Rams Head for a long time but is now known as the Hungry Horse.

Disley is perhaps best known to the visitor as a gateway to Lyme Park (see below) and it is possible to extend this walk to the Park and Hall which are currently managed by The National Trust.

Refreshments

There are several other old hostelries here for this was a watering hole for stage coaches and waggoners before the climb out of the valley on the Old Buxton Road. On the Buxton Road you will also find a tea room.

Nearby Places of Interest

Lyme Hall and Park

This was the home of the Legh family for 600 years and while part of the hall is Elizabethan much of it dates from the past two centuries. It houses several period interiors including a unique collection of English clocks. For many, the joys of Lyme are the extensive parklands where red and fallow deer can be seen. There are also unusual landmarks such as The Cage, a watch tower from which to follow the stag hunts. In front of the hall is the lake, and nearby an orangery and a sunken Dutch garden. There is a shop and cafe at Lyme Hall.

New Mills

Just across the border in Derbyshire is a fine local walk in New Mills down to The Torrs, a gorge which once housed several mills. There is a visitor centre and several well worn paths which make an ideal two hour saunter.

The Walk

1. Begin your walk from Disley railway station and proceed to Fountain Square, by the Hungry Horse. Cross over the road and on the left just up the bank you will see the old Police House on Jackson's Edge Lane. However, cross this and walk ahead to the Dandy Cock, a well established roadside pub in the Robinson's stable.

2. Just before it, go left down Hollinwood Road to pass cottages which date from the late 18th century. The Goyt Valley was a great attraction to industrialists in earlier centuries as there was a plentiful supply of fast running water to feed water and power.

Note the stream and gully to the left and the allotments on the other side. Walk under the bridge and keep ahead. The views across to Mellor Moor and up the valley to New Mills are excellent.

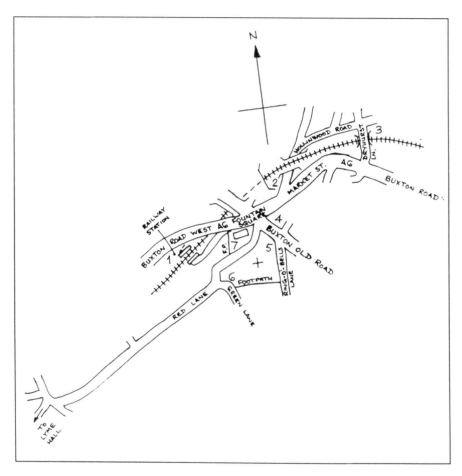

3. At the crossroads go right into Dryhurst Lane which leads back to the Buxton Road by the Albert Hotel. Go right along a crescent to pass The Crescent which has interesting etched glass windows. Cross over when possible before Fountain Square. The fountain was erected by Richard Thomas Orford in 1834 and is protected by iron railings.

4. Go left up the Buxton Old Road. On the opposite side is the Old School House, now a surgery. The church stands behind on a small ridge. Pass by the Mousetrap pub on the left and Malt Cottage on the right, presumably a malt house in earlier times.

5. Cross over to the White Horse Hotel. It is said that the pub at one time housed the bears in its cellars which were used for bear bating in the square. Walk up Ring o' Bells Lane as far as the Quaker House, now a private dwelling. Here a little path drops down right to a stream and up to the perimeter of the churchyard. You can go right to visit the church. Otherwise, keep ahead.

6. The path gives out onto an approach road to the church. Keep ahead to pass an old vicarage and then join another road. Go left if you wish to detour for a mile to Lyme Hall but expect to walk for 2-3 miles. Otherwise, go right and as the road bends right, go ahead through a small gate.

7. The path drops down the hillside to Disley railway station. The wood is quiet and offers surprisingly good views of Disley village.

10. Farndon

Access

Farndon and its sister village of Holt in Wales, not surprisingly lie on the English – Welsh border seven miles south of Chester, just off the A534. A car park lies off Church Lane, next to the Parish Church of St Chad.

The Village

Farndon is a small border village, the bridge across the Dee takes the traveller into Wales, and the town of Holt.

Farndon (Abigail Bristow)

Refreshments

Farndon has several pubs near the river, including the Farndon Arms, a free house, the Nags Head, a Marstons pub, and the Greyhound, all on the main road leading down to the Dee. The authors visited the Greyhound, serving Greenalls Mild and Bitter in very good condition. The bar has a very large geological map of Great Britain on display positioned above a real fire. Animal recognition charts also feature on the walls, which might help you to identify the breed of the next sheep you see.

Nearby Places of Interest

River Dee

The River Dee, meandering north and south of the villages of Farndon and Holt offers a wonderful range of strolls and walks along footpaths, both along the banks of the river, and also within its flood plain.

The Walk

1. From the car park, cross the road and enter the churchyard, the graveyard is just about fully occupied: there are fine views across the river to the church in Holt. The church is red Cheshire sandstone and the churchyard, attractive with yew trees. After a stroll round the church yard, exit and turn left along the road.

2. Turn right, just before Church Court into Church Street, passing to your left a Victorian house of odd design. At the end of Church Street turn left onto the High Street. Walk down the hill past the Farndon Arms, the Nags Head and the Greyhound.

3. Just before the river, turn left onto the riverside footpath (public toilets located here). There is a picnic area, where you can sit and watch the river flow by. Follow the path past the rock exposed by quarrying for local buildings, including the bridge over the river. This area is a geological site of special scientific interest.

Walk on past the Boathouse Restaurant and another curious rockface. The footpath continues along the riverbank, although it can get muddy, it is very beautiful and peaceful. The view across to Holt church – our next destination – is very attractive. Turn back towards the bridge, which is itself worth looking at.

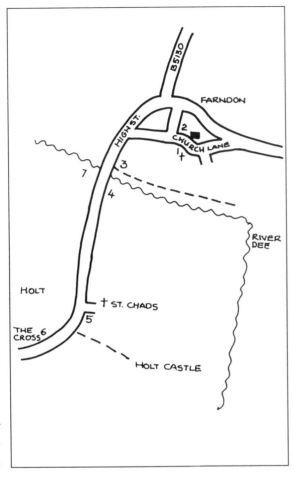

4. Cross the bridge, which offers attractive views up and down the river and find yourself in Clwyd. Follow the road up the hill, past attractive red brick villas, and an antique shop. As you reach the Peal o' Bells, a free house, turn left immediately before it and take the path to St Chad's church. This church too is constructed form red Cheshire sandstone, the graveyard contains memorials for the 18th century. There is a plaque at the rear of the church to Jasper and Amy Pollock, whose deaths are recorded as 1712 and 1740 respectively. The graveyard slopes down towards the river, stopping short of the flood plain. The views back across the river are excellent, with sheep resident in the field adjoining. The church itself dates from 1281, the clock from 1721.

5. On leaving the church continue up the road past Rose Cottage
    (1700). On reaching the post office, the road curves to the right,
    but our path lies down a signed lane to the left. This takes us past
    the Holt Endowed School (1874-1977), now a private dwelling,
    down a muddy lane towards the river. The remains of the castle
    sit perched on a sandstone rock. Although the remains them-
    selves are – at present – fenced off and unsafe to visit, it is possible
    to walk right round the castle. There isn't that much of it left
    standing, but on the river side, a doorway and steps within can
    still be seen. Holt Castle was constructed in the 13th and 14th
    Centuries, falling in 1647 to the Parliamentary forces. The sur-
    rounding grassy area is attractive, with a few flowers even in
    February. Retrace your steps up the path, and continue along the
    road to the Cross.

6. Here stands the war memorial and a much older cross dating from
    1483. There is also a very useful display giving much background
    information about Holt, which was originally a roman settlement.
    The map gives directions for those who wish to visit the site of
    the roman tile works or the castle fish ponds.

7. Return down the road to the river, crossing the bridge back into
    Cheshire. At this point the pubs lining the street provide useful
    refreshment stops. When ready to continue, retrace your steps to,
    the car park.

11. Frodsham

Access

Frodsham is a small town situated in north-west Cheshire on the A56, 10 miles north-east of Chester.

Parking is available on both sides of High Street at SJ515777 and in the car park off Church Street at SJ518777.

Bus services run to and from Chester, Northwich, Runcorn and Warrington. Frodsham is also served by rail with direct services to and from Chester, Liverpool, Manchester, North Wales and Warrington. Full details are obtainable from Cheshire Bus: phone numbers listed in the introduction.

The Town

Frodsham is an old market town whose recorded history goes back to late Saxon times. It is situated on the edge of the west Cheshire sandstone ridge, overlooking the Mersey estuary and Frodsham marshes. Delamere forest once reached the southern edges of Frodsham marshes.

It is thought probable that the main A56 follows an old Roman route between Deva (Chester) and Wilderspool (Warrington). Frodsham was one of the principal manors of Edwin, the last Saxon earl of Mercia. It then belonged to the Norman earls of Chester and, finally, to the Crown. The church dates from the eleventh century and is mentioned in the Domesday Book.

A salt refinery opened in 1694. The salt was brought from Northwich, probably along the River Weaver. Frodsham was once a major port at the mouth of the Weaver. Later the marshes were drained and from the 1720s the river was continuously improved and modernised.

The Cholmondeley Arms (Tom Hornby)

Today, Frodsham is a busy market town as well as being a pleasant dormitory suburb to nearby industrial towns, and to Liverpool.

Refreshments

Frodsham has several interesting old public houses, several of which serve food, particularly at lunchtime. There are also Coffee shops, Bistros and restaurants, including Indian, Italian and Peking Style restaurants, chiefly in the area of Main Street and Church Street.

Nearby Places of Interest

Overton Hill

Above the town, immediately to the south, is Overton Hill, topped by its Memorial Monument. This offers a fine vantage point, with views of the Weaver and Mersey as they flow past Frodsham Marshes. Not so beautiful, but nevertheless of interest, is the panorama of the chemical industry of Cheshire set out before you. Archaeological finds suggest that prehistoric people lived on and around this hill and its neighbour, Helsby Hill.

Mersey Estuary

The Mersey estuary is an almost unprotected area, but is important for wildlife, especially birds. The unromantically named sludge lagoons at Frodsham are one of the best places to access the estuary. Shelduck, widgeon, teal and pintail are among the birds to be seen there in winter.

Sandstone Trail

The 'Sandstone Trail' starts from Overton Hill and runs southwards towards Delamere Forest.

The Walk

1. Start from the bottom of Church Street where it joins Main Street and High Street at SJ516779. On the corner of Church Street and Main Street is the Golden Lion, a pleasant pub with several rooms. Across the road is the Bears Paw public house, built of sandstone in 1632 as a Coaching Inn and mail collection point.

2. Set off up Church Street, Frodsham's main shopping street. Just before the railway bridge, on the right, note the unusual phone box with integral post-box marked GR and then the Cholmondeley Arms, a black and white public house with handsome stained glass windows, built in 1897. Here, also, is the station; The railway was opened in 1850.

3. Go under the railway bridge. On the right is the old National School building dating from 1835. This was one of the voluntary schools which provided primary education to the less well off before the Education Act of 1870. National Schools were founded by the Anglican Society. They were aided by a small grant from 1833 and remained the only schools in many villages after the 1870 Act. Just beyond it is Kydds Public House, an Ale House. A little further on, the shops give way to housing.

4. As Church Street runs uphill, it cuts into the rock with the houses high above the road, especially on the left where the houses are

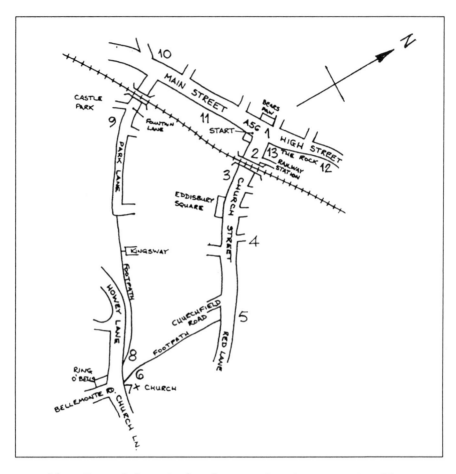

older. One of these is dated 1781. Continue, passing Kingsway on your right.

5. Shortly after passing Churchfield Road on the right Church Street becomes Red Lane. Here a footpath leads to the right up some steps. It is signposted 'Delamere Way and Stretton Heath 33 km'. Follow this straight, paved path uphill between hedges. After a distance of about two hundred yards you reach a sandstone wall on the left, which is the boundary of the churchyard. The path follows the wall and eventually bears left. Continue, and turn left through gates into the grounds of St Laurence's church.

6. St Laurence's was originally Norman but was restored between 1880 and 1883, when its appearance was very much altered. Late Norman work and fragments of Saxon crosses can be seen inside. The porches are early eighteenth century. The bee carved on the church is in memory of William Cotton, Vicar of St Laurence's 1857-79, who was a bee fancier and introduced the honey bee to New Zealand. He was a colourful local figure, travelling with a parrot called Papagay, and he had a Maori welcome inscribed on the front doorstep of the Vicarage. The bee is also used on the badge of the local school.

7. Leave the south porch, passing the sundial to reach Church Road. Ahead is the Ring O'Bells, an old public house with fascinating little rooms, low beamed ceilings and beer served from hand pumps. Lunches are served here and there is a beer garden. To your left along Church Road, beyond the churchyard, Church House Farm is worth a diversion.

8. From the church gate turn right into Howey Lane. The pavement leads straight ahead and diverges from Howey Lane which drops away to your left. Cross the green, admiring the panorama of the estuary and the vibrant industry of the district. Shortly you arrive at some steps which lead down between hedges. Continue downhill, along the paved path, passing Kingsway on your right. The path leads you into Park Lane, a twentieth century residential road. After passing Princeway on the right, continue ahead into Fountain Lane.

9. On your left is a handsome brick structure, formerly an outbuilding, now converted to housing. Between this building and the railway bridge is the entrance to Castle Park, where there are sports facilities, gardens, galleries, craft workshops, coffee and gift shops and a children's playground. The clock on the former stable block is kept three minutes fast at the request of the former owner, Edward Abbott Wright. Continue under the railway bridge, passing two tiny old cottages to reach Main Street again. Here turn right.

10. Main Street is an old fashioned street, wide and tree-lined. On

Thursdays a market is held here. There has been a weekly market since 1661. The street has many interesting and attractive old buildings, including Ashley House, built about 1830. Further on, also to the left, is the Old Hall Hotel, a handsome building with thatched cottages next door. Opposite the hotel is an old, wooden framed house.

11. Further along Main Street, on the right, is the Queens Head Hotel, a seventeenth century Inn and the oldest public building in Frodsham. A tiny old shop is tucked in next door. A plaque on the Queens Head informs the visitor that the Court Leet of the Manor and, later, the Parish Council, met in a room at the rear. The old sandstone stables can still be seen at the back.

12. For those who wish to explore further, cross the end of Church Street into High Street. Ahead is 'The Rock', a sandstone outcrop. Several interesting old cottages stand here, built directly onto the rock. Notice Cave Cottage and Old Cottage with a plaque dating it at 1580. Leading up the side of Old Cottage are some steps from which you can see that the house is wooden-framed.

13. Return to the bottom of Church Street and the start of the walk.

12. Gawsworth

Access

Gawsworth lies three miles to the south west of Macclesfield, just off the busy A536 to Congleton. It must be one of the prettiest villages in East Cheshire and certainly exhibits a rich variety of architecture within a square half mile of land. Those seeking to park without intrusion will park just south of the Harrington Arms at a lay-by known as Gandysbrook, because of the trickle of water which flows nearby. There is a telephone kiosk here too (SJ885691).

Gawsworth is easy to get to by bus from Macclesfield, Congleton and Crewe. The service is hourly and runs every day, including from mid-day on Sundays and through until late evening. This makes it an attractive alternative to the car as a call at the Harrington Arms is almost obligatory.

The Village

Gawsworth is as nearly an archetypal corner of old England, with its fine fish pools, manor house and church alongside, not to mention the farm-cum pub standing handsomely at the end of a row of fine trees. Cows graze in the surrounding pastures and of an evening can be heard bellowing in the stillness of dusk. This tranquillity tends to be broken only on concert nights at Gawsworth Hall, an enjoyable affair all round, except for the traffic jams afterwards.

Notice that recent development is a good quarter of a mile away at what is known on the maps as Warren but tends to be called Gawsworth too. The oldest part here is at the crossroads and small village green, otherwise it is predominantly new housing.

Gawsworth Hall

Refreshments

The Harrington Arms is unusual on two counts. Firstly, it is one of very few remaining farm-cum-pubs left in England and secondly it has not given over to the serving of food at the expense of all else. Step back in time here for the landlady serves traditional Robinson's beers on hand pull from a small bar to the right of the entrance. On the left is a room not much touched over the decades where folk happens on Friday nights and at other times people enjoy the simplicity of the settles and benches – no music or gambling machines in sight!

Nearby Places of Interest

Footpaths

There is a well-kept network of paths from the village, including walks to North Rode and to Fool's Nook which is inextricably linked with the folklore of Gawsworth. On the Marton Road you will find a garden centre.

The Walk

1. Start from the Harrington Arms. From the pub entrance go left. Cross the junction and keep ahead along the tree-lined road up to the church. You will note the path on the right beforehand leading off to North Rode. Walk up the steps to the churchyard and church itself.

2. Continue through the churchyard and cut left to a small lychgate. This stands on the dam between pools. The one to your right is still full but to appreciate how it adds to the setting you need to turn right onto the road. There stands Gawsworth Hall, an imposing building.

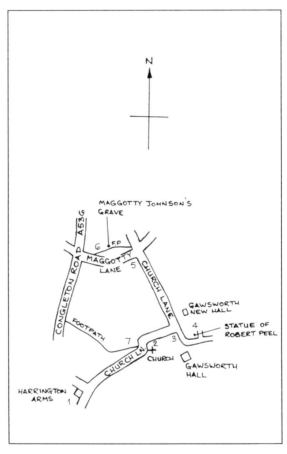

3. At the corner go right and walk towards the gates of the hall. A tour is preferable to a few words in a book. It is steeped in historical interest but at the same time surprisingly homely.

4. If not visiting then just walk left for a few metres; here on your left is a most welcome guest in the village, a statue of Peel in his prime, with no real interpretation, simply a slab of stone adjacent which announces his surname. Retrace your steps to the corner and now keep ahead. On the right is the new Gawsworth Hall, dating incidentally from 1712 and now a Grade II listed building which has been converted into luxury apartments.

5. Walk up Church Lane to the crossroads with Maggotty Lane. Cross over and enter the woodland on the left, owned by the National Trust. A little path leads up to the grave of Maggotty Johnson, who according to the records was an entertainer at Gawsworth Hall and a good one at that. The trouble is that his contemporaries were somewhat disconcerted at his bawdiness and here he lies rather than in the parish churchyard. The proof lies in the words on his tomb which in themselves are lewd.

6. The path leads through the woods down to Maggotty Lane. Go right to the main road. Then turn left to walk along the pavement for no more than 200 metres when you will see a footpath sign on the left. Walk up the steps and cross the stile. Keep company with the hedge as it climbs to a brow and then dips down to another stile. Go over this and bear slightly right to stroll around to the dam of another pool, which has been without water for many years. Go left up to a stile and exit onto a road by the church.

7. Turn right and retrace your steps back down to the Harrington Arms. This section used to be the main road and you can imagine the scene when waggoners and coaches pulled up outside to draw refreshment from the cellar. Even a decade ago the Crosville bus was known to draw up outside and wait for the occasional customer to rush out of the door at the last minute. Now you have to walk down the road on the right to bus stops at the junction.

13. Great Budworth

Access

Great Budworth (SJ665775) is in north Cheshire, two miles north of Northwich just to the east of the A559. The village does not have a car park but space for parking can often be found on High Street.

Bus services run to and from Northwich and Warrington. Alight on Northwich Road near its junction with High Street. Full details are obtainable from Cheshire Bus: phone numbers listed in the introduction.

The Village

Great Budworth is a picturesque village with many interesting old buildings and is a popular location for films and TV dramas. Situated on a hill, it overlooks Budworth Mere. The White Hart, Ring O'Bells and Saracen's head are former ale-houses now converted to private homes.

It was one of the largest parishes in England at the time of the Norman invasion and in the middle ages it remained second in importance only to Prestbury.

On 11 November each year there is a wake to commemorate the building of the church. Comberbach Mummers perform the local soulcaking play and traditionally flummery (frumenty) is eaten. This is made from boiled wheat, milk sugar and spice.

Refreshments

Food is available at the George and Dragon public house. A little further north along Northwich Road is another pub, The Cock o' Budworth.

Nearby Places of Interest

Arley Hall

Arley Hall opens to the public and is situated about two miles north-east of Great Budworth.

Lion Salt Works

The Lion Salt Works is an old open-pan salt works, maintained as an industrial museum. It is in Marston, about 1½ miles south of Great Budworth.

A cottage in High Street, Great Budworth (Tom Hornby)

The Walk

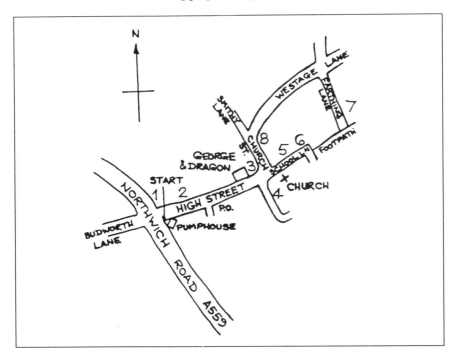

1. The walk starts from the crossroads where High Street meets Northwich Road (A559). The small building on the corner is a Pumphouse. This was built in 1869 by Rowland Eyles Egerton Warburton, the "Rhyming Poet of Arley," who wrote the verses which appear on the Pumphouse. Water was obtained from the pump until 1934. The road here is overhung by large trees.

2. Set off up High Street. After a short distance you enter the village. Note the wooden-framed house on a sandstone base to the left, built in 1706. The other houses in the village are mostly of brick. On the right just before the Post Office is Bakery Cottage which has ornate plaster work on its upper storey. The Post Office itself is an old brick building with interesting ornamental brick work and shutters over the ground floor windows.

3. At the centre of the village, across the road from the church, is the George and Dragon Hotel. Note the verses carved into the fencing at the front of the pub; This is more work by "The Rhyming Poet of Arley."

4.   The church of St Mary's dates from the 14th century. Built in Perpendicular style with a low-pitched cambered tie-beam roof with panelling, it was one of several constructed in Cheshire during this period. The north arcade is in Decorated style and the south is Perpendicular. The tower was the last part of the church to be completed, between 1500 and 1520. Towers were a particularly notable feature of Cheshire churches. Outside the church gate are the stocks, which were used up to 1854 to discourage vagrants. To obtain a better view of the church, turn right down South Bank.

5.   Return to High Street and turn right into School Lane, a picturesque cobbled street which runs between old terraced cottages and the churchyard. At the end of the terrace you can look back along the side wall and see the old wooden frame with brick infill.

6.   You now reach a school on the left-hand side and here the cobbled surface becomes a dirt track. Pass the school to reach a wicket gate and continue along the path with a row of trees on each side. To the left are playing fields and after a short distance there are open fields to the right. Pass through the wooden stile and turn left here into Farthing Lane, an unsurfaced track.

7.   Follow Farthing Lane to reach Westage Lane. Turn left into Westage Lane which leads towards the village centre. On the right-hand side are modern buildings styled to blend in with the older architecture. The slightly earlier homes to the left make fewer concessions to the past. The whole area is pleasantly lined with many trees and hedges.

8.   Soon you reach the older part of the village once more and the road curves left into Church Street. Here pretty old cottages nestle close to the road and the church is visible between them. Continuing, you again reach High Street which leads back to the start of the walk.

14. Knutsford

Access

Knutsford is a very attractive old town in the north of mid-Cheshire on the A50 where it is joined by the A5033 and the A537. It is six miles north-east of Northwich and a similar distance west of Wilmslow. There is a large car park off Stanley Road, behind the Council Offices and Tourist Information Centre at SJ751784.

Bus services run to and from Altrincham, Northwich, Macclesfield, Wilmslow and, on certain days, Congleton and Warrington. Alight at the bus station. Knutsford is served directly by rail from Chester, Northwich, Altrincham, Stockport, Manchester and many other towns in the North West. Full details are obtainable from

Marble Arch, King Street, Knutsford (Tom Hornby)

Cheshire Bus: phone numbers are listed in the introduction to this book.

The Town

The name Knutsford may be derived from "neat's ford": a place where cattle were driven across. Others believe that it comes from "Canute's ford" – the place where that king crossed the river Lily on his way to fight the Scots. The name is of Scandinavian character, as are many others in the area, such as Toft, the Peovers and Tabley.

A major administrative centre for Cheshire in Norman times, Knutsford continued to be important through the Middle Ages and into modern times. The town's Sessions house is still used as a County Court.

Knutsford has cottages dating from the 16th century. It also boasts several timber framed buildings and a fine collection of town houses from the 18th century. Countryside and open spaces come right into the town.

The town is best known as the basis for Mrs Gaskell's book 'Cranford', a classic picture of old Knutsford society. Mrs Elizabeth Gaskell lived here for many years and attended the Unitarian Chapel.

Refreshments

Knutsford is well provided with public houses, cafes and restaurants, some of which will be mentioned in the description of the walk.

Nearby Places of Interest

Tatton Hall

Immediately to the north is Tatton Park with the Hall and Mere. The grounds extend almost into the centre of Knutsford and therefore permit a pleasant and easy ramble, using made roads or footpaths, directly from the shops. In the grounds, at SJ756813, can be found the remains of an early Roman or Anglo-Saxon timber long-house and associated outbuildings, fences and palisades. There is also a complex of Mediaeval buildings. Tatton Hall Museum has some interesting local exhibits.

Mobberley

The nearby village of Mobberley, the largest Parish in England, is also the birthplace of George Leigh Mallory, the climber who was lost with Andrew Irvine near the summit of Everest in 1924. There is a memorial to him in Mobberley church.

The Walk

1. The walk starts from Toft Road at SJ752786 in front of the Parish Church of St John the Baptist. The church was built between 1741 and 1744 of brick with stone dressings and is now surrounded by fine trees. The church contains many interesting features including windows depicting images of Daniel kneeling and Joshua and Aaron with Moses as a battle rages. The font, carved with elaborate scenes, dates from 1864.

2. After visiting the church and churchyard, turn right from Toft Road into Church Hill. The ornate red brick building on the corner to your left is the old Town Hall, constructed in 1872. It is now occupied by a furniture store and Knutsford Post Office. Follow this picturesque cobbled street downhill. At the bottom of Church Hill turn left into King Street.

3. King Street is Knutsford's main shopping street and has much to offer the visitor. On your left is the rather odd Gaskell Memorial Tower and Kings Coffee House, later used as Knutsford Urban District Council Offices, and now accommodating cafes and restaurants. These buildings were commissioned by the eccentric Richard Harding Watt. Among the varied small shops are many restaurants, coffee shops and several public houses and hotels. Much of the street dates from the eighteenth century. The Royal George Hotel is a coaching inn with a cobbled carriageway leading through the building. Further along, next door to the

White Lion public house, is the Penny Farthing Museum and several black and white timber framed buildings.

4. On the corner of Minshull Street and King Street is The Angel, a particularly fine old coaching inn. Continue along King Street. On your right you will find Marble Arch with a view through to the cobbled street with its pretty whitewashed cottages. A little further along King Street is the old Post Office building. Notice the sundial on the front.

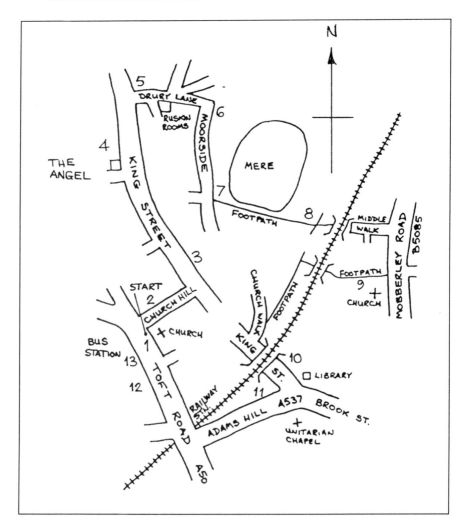

5. A short distance further on turn right into Drury Lane which leads downhill. Ahead are the Ruskin Rooms, a recreation and reading room for the people of Knutsford, erected in 1902 by Richard Harding Watt in his usual Latin style. It was later used as a fire station. Continue downhill alongside a terrace of houses which have a very Mediterranean air.

6. At the bottom of the hill, turn right onto a rougher track. To the right are modern houses and flats in an Italian style which harmonises well with the buildings in Drury lane. The area of reeds on the left is part of Tatton Mere.

7. After a short distance the track becomes surfaced. Here a narrow road leads to the right, but the walk takes a left turn, onto a paved footpath. Follow this path between the Mere and the park. The Mere is a designated Site of Special Scientific Interest, being one of the largest areas of fen and reed swamps in Cheshire. A notice has been erected describing the many species of birds which may be seen here.

8. Ahead another church is visible above the trees. Follow the path ahead, passing under the Manchester to Chester railway line, to Middle Walk, a pleasant residential road which leads uphill. Note the particularly fine terraced cottages to your left with their ornate brickwork. Continue to the junction with the B5085, Mobberley Road. Here turn right and after a short distance, just before you reach the red-brick church, take a footpath which leads to the right between walls and hedges, alongside the churchyard.

9. Follow the path downhill, through a pleasant park, once again passing under the railway. Immediately after emerging from under the bridge, turn left onto a wider pathway. On your right is the park. The path joins a minor road called Church Walk. Continue ahead along Church Walk, and then turn left into King Street and pass under the railway.

10. Follow King Street the few yards to its junction with Brook Street and Adams Hill, which form part of the busy A537. To your left, on Brook Street, is the Public Free Library. On the other side of the main road stands the Unitarian Chapel, built in 1689. Here Mrs Gaskell was buried in 1865.

11. Turn right and ascend Adams Hill, with the railway station to your right. At the traffic lights, turn right to rejoin Toft Road. To your left is the old council chamber, now used as a tourist information office. A little further along on the right is the modern Civic Centre and Studio Cinema.

12. The most imposing building in this area is the Sessions House which you see on your left, still used as a County Court. Between 1559 and 1660, Knutsford was one of five towns in Cheshire where sessions of the peace were held. The site behind the Sessions House was occupied by Knutsford County Goal, which was built in 1818 and was the site of at least seven executions. Its use as a criminal prison ceased after 1914, however, and the building was demolished in 1934.

13. Continue the short distance along Toft Road to reach the church and the start of the walk.

15. Langley and Sutton

Access

There is a regular bus from Macclesfield every day except Sunday. Those travelling by car should take a left turn at a junction on the Leek Road in Macclesfield as signposted. There is very limited parking in Langley, so please be considerate.

Bottoms Reservoir (Norman James)

The Villages

Nestling at the foot of Tegg's Nose Country Park, at the edge of Macclesfield Forest, Langley village lies just a few miles from Macclesfield. Flowing alongside the village is the River Bollin, which at one time provided power and water for up to five mills built to manufacture silk and buttons. In 1826 William Smith of Nottingham, developed Langley Mill from a cottage industry. It eventually became the biggest silk printing, dyeing and finishing works in the world.

Pretty terraced cottages, some with upper garret rooms where home workers wove the silk, line the main street and the village pub is in the very middle, the St Dunstan. The cottages almost reach up as far as the four reservoirs, built to supply the people of Macclesfield from 1850-1929. The reservoirs provide a home for an enormous variety of birds, some of which are depicted in the famous paintings of Charles Tunnicliffe, who was born in Langley.

Sutton is larger than Langley but they virtually flow into one another. In the nineteenth century the village prospered for many decades from the local silk industry. One of the main mills, Sutton Lane Ends, provided employment until its closure in the 1870s. It has since been demolished. The Macclesfield Canal sweeps through Sutton. In the direction of Macclesfield, at Gurnett, is the site of the millwright's shop where James Brindley, the famous canal engineer served his apprenticeship. Across the road from here lies Sutton Hall which dates from 1520. Though it has known several uses in its time it now serves as a pub, restaurant, and hotel, complete with four poster beds!

Refreshments

There are no shops in Langley, but there is a general store and post office in Sutton. The following pubs are on the walk – St Dunstan's, The Church Inn, The Lamb Inn, Sutton Hall, and The Old King's Head. There is a garden centre at Gurnett.

Nearby Places of Interest

Macclesfield Forest

Langley is close to Macclesfield Forest. See the notes in the Macclesfield chapter. Tegg's Nose Country Park is a short but steep climb from the village.

The Walk

1. From the St Dunstan Inn, go left to walk along the main road. Here you will see a fine collection of weaver's cottages on the left. Go left at the junction into Holehouse Lane. To the left is the site of Bollin Head Mill but there is no trace now of this building. The road rises up to a junction between two reservoirs. These are the smaller of the group of four mentioned above. Tegg's Nose Reservoir (on the left) was built in 1871, and at a maximum depth of 37 feet has a capacity of 24.5 million gallons. Bottoms (on the right) was built 21 years earlier and with a maximum depth of 32 feet has a capacity of 34 million gallons. They both attract a wide variety of birdlife.

2. Go right here down the steps and along the perimeter of Bottoms reservoir. This is part of the Gritstone Trail, a regional walking route between Lyme Hall and Rushton Spencer. Exit on the road by a group of pretty cottages. Go right to return to the village. Note the old School Board building on the left.

3. Pass by the St Dunstan and at the corner keep right. On the left is a Methodist chapel dating from 1818 but having been rebuilt in 1858, one of many to be found in this area. Cross Coalpit Lane, the name referring to earlier excavations on the hillside. Pass the Working Mens Institute (now known as the Langley Institute). Opposite is the old print works and one of the owners, William Whiston, had the Institute built in the 1880s to educate his work-force.

4. You soon pass Langley Hall, a beautifully restored late 17th

century hall
with a perfect
Queen Anne
doorway. Be-
hind it, to the
right, is another
works, built as a
steam laundry at
the turn of the
century but then
converted to tex-
tile production.
Opposite, a
group of cottages
remains, built
originally for lo-
cal workers.

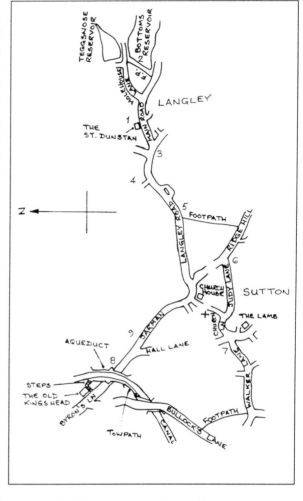

5. Continue along
Main Road until
you reach a
group of more
modern houses
on the left. Go
left as sign-
posted between
two houses and
walk up through
the fields to-
wards Ridge Hill. Go right down the road until you come to
Ridgehill Farm.

6. Go left along Judy Lane to Sutton where you join Church Lane.
To the right you can see the church standing on high ground.
Near the junction was at one time Sutton Lane End Mill which
specialised in silk throwing. It is now demolished. Go left and
walk to the cross roads at the centre of the village. To the left is
The Lamb Inn.

7. Go ahead along Walker Lane until you reach the junction with Parvey Lane. You will pass on the right a farm where Charles Tunnicliffe, the famous artist, lived. There is a plaque to commemorate this. Go right over a stile here to walk across a field to Bullocks Lane. Pass the entrance to Sutton Hall. Go over the canal bridge and turn right to walk along a towpath. Cross the Gurnett aqueduct. Go left down steps to the road by The Old King's Head pub.

8. Turn left to walk under the canal and by a number of interesting buildings dating from a similar era. On Plough House there is a commemorative stone which reads:
"On these premises James Brindley, famous Civil Engineer and Canal Builder served as apprentice to Abraham Bennett."

9. Go left at the junction into Jarman. On the right is the remains of what looks to be a pound of some description where stray animals would have been kept. Follow the Langley Road back to Langley village keeping left by the well located Church Inn.

16. Lymm

Access

L ymm is in the north of the County, four miles east of Warrington on the A6144 at its junction with the A56. There is ample car parking in the centre of the town by the Public Library and the canal at SJ681873.

Bus services run to and from Warrington and Altrincham. Alight in the village centre, near The Cross. Full details are obtainable from Cheshire Bus: phone numbers listed in the introduction.

The Village

Lymm is an attractive small town, with a village-like atmosphere. The first known sign of settlement in the area is a flint from the late Neolithic or Early Bronze Period. The town is known to have existed in Norman times. Today it provides pleasant housing for many people who work in Warrington or Manchester

Refreshments

There is an abundance of refreshment facilities. In addition to the four pubs mentioned in the walk, there is a chip shop, a Bistro and several restaurants offering English, Italian and Indian cuisine.

Lymm Bridge (Tom Hornby)

Nearby Places of Interest

Dunham Park

Three miles to the east of Lymm is Dunham Park with deer roaming among the trees. Dunham Hall dates from about 1720.

Warburton

The picturesque little village of Warburton, about two miles north-west of Lymm, is well worth a visit.

The Walk

1. The walk commences from Bridgewater Street, near the fine red brick Post Office building at SJ682873. Opposite the Post Office, and ascending almost parallel to Bridgewater Street, is Legh Street. Follow its cobbles the few yards to reach the Bridgewater Canal. The canal was built by the famous engineer Thomas

Brindley for the Duke of Bridgewater. Completed in 1777, its function was to carry coal from his mines near Manchester to Liverpool for export.

2. Turn right along the paved and fenced path which follows the canal. The pretty brick and sandstone arch of Lymm Bridge is reached after about 100 yards. Divert momentarily to your left onto the bridge. Note the picturesque terrace of cottages to the left, built largely of sandstone, and the view ahead out of the town to fields and hills.

3. Turn back towards the town centre. The road here is known as The Cross. Pass the Bulls Head to your left. This has a lounge and a public bar and serves food at lunch-time. A little further on is the Golden Fleece, a larger building to your right. It is an old pub which has been nicely modernised and also provides lunches.

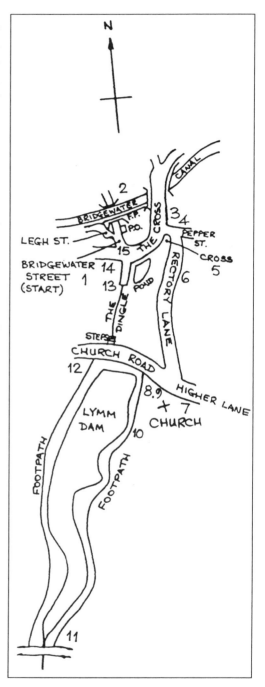

4. Continuing, note on your left the fine old shop front of the premises occupied by the Trattoria Baci restaurant. Next door, just into Pepper Street, is a Pizzeria.

5. Cross the road to view the impressive sandstone cross, built on a sandstone outcrop. This monument was restored in 1897 by public subscription on Queen Victoria's Diamond Jubilee. In front stands a fully functional stocks, and benches on which to relax and enjoy the village atmosphere.

6. Leaving the Cross, your way is now along Rectory Lane. This has no name sign, but its entry is easily identified to the right behind the Cross, at right angles to Pepper Street. This lane runs between sandstone walls, pleasantly over-hung by trees from both sides. Pass Dingle Hotel on the right. Continue, with more modern houses on each side. Shortly, you will reach a junction with the main A56 road, here known as Church Road.

7. To your left on the other side of Church Road is the Church Green public house. This large building has a single open lounge bar and serves food all day. Ahead and to your right, partially hidden by trees, is St Mary's Parish Church, constructed of sandstone. It was rebuilt during the last century. With its square tower it is an imposing landmark. An inspection of the church is recommended as it has some fine stained glass windows and a pulpit dating from 1623. Lymm church was one of those established by the Normans and is known to have been in existence by 1291, when the Ecclesiastical Taxation of England and Wales was made by Pope Nicholas IV.

8. The walk continues to the right along Church Road. After a few yards you will reach Lymm Dam on your left. This beautiful setting is semi-natural and was created between 1821 and 1824 by the damming of Bradley Brook to allow the main road, now the A56, to cross the valley. It is a favourite haunt of anglers and bird watchers. The water also provided power for mills in the centre of the town. Early this century Lord Leverhulme, better known for the garden village of Port Sunlight near Ellesmere Port, proposed an ambitious landscaping scheme, but it came to nothing – and it is hard to see how the area could have been improved!

9.   Here, beside the main road, are toilet facilities. At this point too, a choice of routes presents itself. Those who do not wish to take the walk round the lake can continue along Church Road across the dam, which offers a fine view along the valley. At the far end of the dam cross the road to the public footpath, known as The Dingle, which leads down to the village. The walk around the lake will bring you back to this spot.

10.   If you are taking the walk round the lake, turn left off the road onto a well made path, just before reaching the dam. Here you will pass a picnic area with tables and benches which overlook the water. The lake lies in a valley cut out of sandstone and in many places is fringed with reeds. Follow the path, which is quite well maintained but can be muddy in wet weather. After a while the path turns left up a flight of steps reinforced with timber. Continue some distance through large trees. As the far end of the lake is reached, fields are just visible through the trees to your left and the path is joined by wooden railings from the left.

11.   The path bears to the right and reaches a wide track. Pass through the wooden stile, crossing the impressive bridge to your right. Immediately on reaching the far end of the bridge, turn to the right through another wooden stile and onto a footpath. You will now be heading northwards through trees, back towards Lymm. Presently, the path splits. Follow either route, for they come together again a short distance further on. The lake is once again clearly visible to your right. Continuing, the path rejoins the lake shore. The church can soon be seen across the water; a lovely view, especially in the evening with the lake in shadow and the church and trees opposite caught by the sun. Eventually, a stone wall appears to your left and, shortly afterwards, the dam and Church Road are reached.

12.   Cross the main road and take the signed footpath opposite, The Dingle. This leads down stone steps between iron railings. Here you are surrounded by large trees populated by many grey squirrels. These seem quite used to people and will sit and watch you pass. Follow the path past amazing tree roots clambering over the exposed rock. To your right runs Bradley Brook, in which fish may be seen.

13. After about a quarter of a mile, the village is reached. The view, as you enter the village, is quite lovely. To your left are houses built of sandstone, set into a ledge cut into the natural rock. A small weir holds back the brook to your right, with picturesque cottages on the other side. Notice the ornate brick building in front of you which houses the Village Bakery.

14. Follow the pavement left into Eagle Brow. Here you will find the Spread Eagle public house. Its entrance is wide, with level access from the pavement, ideal for wheelchairs. Do not be put off by the slightly forbidding exterior. The interior, you will find, is most impressive and with a friendly atmosphere. A central bar serves several rooms. At the foot of the stairs leading to the ballroom is a glass case containing a stuffed eagle.

15. To complete the walk, cross Eagle Brow and re-enter Bridgwater Street, the starting point.

17. Macclesfield

Access

Macclesfield (SJ918735) is well served by trains and buses from nearby towns, especially Stockport and Manchester. There is a daily service from most areas although bus services across the county to the west are sparse. There are several car parks in the town but they are very busy. Parking near the bus and rail stations is particularly difficult.

The Town

Macclesfield's central core is medieval. Witness the street pattern, around the parish church of St Michael beginning at the market square and down to Church Street, along Chestergate and Jordangate. It is most probable that the 108 steps and Brunswick Hill were planned out during these times as links between a higher town and lower living quarter. Macclesfield had a castle too. Its scant remains were demolished, almost unbelievably, earlier in this century to make way for shops on Mill Street.

Macclesfield was granted a charter in 1261 and has always been host to fairs and markets. It was not until the 18th century that early industrialisation began to shape the rest of the town. Small scale mills grew up around the River Bollin, mainly in the Park Green area. The names of Brocklehurst, Roe and Smales are well known to the town, past entrepreneurs who sought to make a fortune from silk manufacture. For 150 years silk production dominated life in Macclesfield and this is reflected in many quarters near to the Bollin.

Macclesfield Sunday School (Nina Mensch)

Refreshments

The town has several cafes and restaurants, especially on the western end of Chestergate. There are dozens of pubs too. Those who enjoy a good pint of traditional ale should head for the Waters Green Tavern in Waters Green, near to the railway station.

Nearby Places of Interest

Tegg's Nose

Tegg's Nose Country Park lies in the hilly borders of Cheshire to the east of Macclesfield. It is a most unusual country park in that its gritstone mother-rock was actively quarried until the 1950s. In half an hour you can be walking to the summit where there are exceptional views.

Macclesfield Forest

Macclesfield Forest was once a Royal Hunting Forest covering the area from Marple to Bosley. "Forest" in bygone days referred to an area of land subject to Forest Law. They were not necessarily tree covered as the modern day word suggests. Since medieval times the area has been cultivated increasingly for agricultural purposes. The present area of woodland is a large plantation belonging to North West Water; the main trees grown are pine, spruce and larch. There are several easy forest walks and the reservoirs attract a variety of water-loving birds.

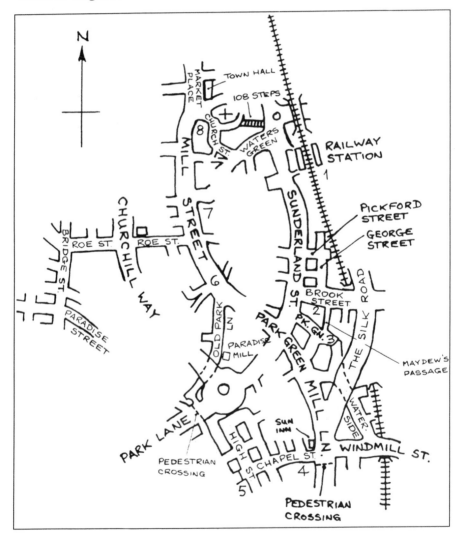

The Walk

1. From Macclesfield Railway Station go left into Sunderland Street and then next left into Pickford Street. Turn right along George Street. On the left is Smales Mill, a good example of a small mill by the Bollin.

2. Cross Brook Street and just on the left is Maydew's Passage. This brings you to Park Green by way of an arch. The building immediately on the left was an engineer and mill furnisher. There are splendid houses here and the Georgian Mill (1785), now owned by Gradus, is a reminder of the early days of silk production. On the corner of Sunderland Street is Park Green House, at one time a rectory and now a doctor's surgery. Note the curved gables and venetian style windows.

3. Go left in Park Green to pass the side of the mill and a little bridge over the Bollin. Go right along Waterside. This gives you a very clear impression of how the mills hugged the water's edge. At Windmill Street (there was originally a windmill at the top end of the street) turn right down to Mill Lane. Cross over the main road at the pedestrian crossing then look back at the building opposite, a classic example of a weaver's cottage with garret windows at the top of the building to allow daylight into a room where the loom was kept.

4. Go left before the Sun public house up Chapel Street. The street is aptly named, as there are fine examples of chapels here.

5. At the end go right along High Street. At the end of the street go left and cross Park Lane at the pedestrian crossing. Walk down what remains of old Park Lane under the new road to Paradise Mill on your right, which illustrates the craftsmanship involved in the production of silk through working exhibits and machines. Then walk by the Old Chadwick Free Library and Art School on your right.

6. Keep ahead to Mill Street. Turn left into Roe Street for the Silk Heritage Centre which is housed in The Sunday School, thought

to have had been used by up to 2500 children at any given time. You can make a detour to Paradise Street from here. Go right to cross the Churchill Way into the continuation of Roe Street. At the crossroads turn left up Bridge Street and you come across beautifully restored weavers' cottages at Paradise Street. Retrace your steps.

7. Walk back along Roe Street to Mill Street and go left to walk through the shopping area to the Town Hall and parish church in Market Square. The truncated cross still stands in the centre but the eye cannot help but concentrate on the Greek Revival style Town Hall (1823) with its modern extension. Alongside is the church of St Michael which dates originally from the 13th century although it was mostly rebuilt in the 18th century and at the beginning of the 20th century. The fine chapel, seen on the right, and referred to as the Savage Chapel, is 16th century. It was built for the Archbishop of York, Thomas Savage in the early 1500s. It contains many effigies of the Savage family.

8. Walk down Church Street to Waters Green or you can cut left by the church for a good view to the hills and the Arighi Bianchi house furnishers below. Then walk down the 108 steps. Time now to refresh yourself – see the refreshments section!

18. Malpas

Access

The very beautiful south Cheshire town of Malpas lies 10 miles east of Wrexham, one mile and a half to the west of the A41. There is a car park in the centre of the town, signposted off the main street.

Regular bus services link Malpas with the following principal locations: Chester, Whitchurch and Tattenhall. Full service details are available from the Cheshire Busline on 01244 602666.

The Town

Malpas (SJ487472) is an attractive south Cheshire town, dominated by the church of St Oswald which lies on a knoll in the centre; the town streets curve around the raised churchyard; there are interesting buildings to be espied throughout the town centre, including the remains of a motte and bailey castle, a 17th century tithe barn, an 18th century school house and a Victorian market cross. There are many fine inns within the town centre, and as the old saying goes: "Malpas ales and Malpas gales cheer the farmer, fill his pails."

Refreshments

A number of fine pubs and inns exist in Malpas, and these are mentioned in the text. Also worthy of note is the Market House Restaurant in Church Street.

Victorian Market Cross, Malpas (Norman James)

Nearby Places of Interest

Footpaths to Threapwood and Sarn

There are several pleasant footpaths leading from Malpas; one of the finest leads you across the fields to Threapwood, and allows you to visit the very fine public house at Sarn, the Queens Head, right on the Welsh border.

Cholmondely Castle

Cholmondely Castle lies close to Malpas and is worth a visit.

The Walk

1. This town trail starts at the Victorian market cross which lies right in the centre at the junction between Church Street and Old Hall Street. The cross is very fine, and very large. Close to the Cross lies the Crown Hotel; opposite lies with Red Lion, which boasts a chair sat upon by King James I. Further along the road in a southerly direction lie many fine timber framed black and white facaded buildings which are worth a look.

2. Turn down Church Street in the direction of the imposing church of St Oswald. This is the B5069 to Wrexham. There are several historical buildings of note along this fine street. To your left lies the Old Vaults public house, and further along opposite the church almshouses dating from 1721 (and from 1955!). To your right lies J Wycherly and Sons, who make saddles and ironmongery: you can see their shop/studio through the archway. The imposing Market House restaurant lies further along to the right: you are advised to book in advance if you wish to eat here. Most of the pubs in Malpas will serve you with food or snacks. Just beyond the Market House is a flight of steps leading up to the church of St Oswald. There are extremely attractive views from this fine churchyard over the surrounding countryside, and indeed over the town of Malpas itself. Wherever you walk in Malpas, new vistas open up through archways and at junctions.

An attractive war memorial stands in front of the churchyard. Note the fine sundial over the church door, as well as the gargoyles and the ornate drainpipes and water conduits.

3. Make your way down the steps from the churchyard at the other side, and continue to walk along Church street: you will come across more beautiful timber-framed buildings to your right, and the view will gradually open out over the fields towards the Welsh border: looking back you will now have a fine view of Malpas and the church on the grassy knoll.

4. Turn back towards the church, pass to the back of the church and take the footpath leading directly over the grass which leads you north; this path leads you through the back-ways of Malpas; turn to the right when you reach a footpath junction, and you will find yourself back on the High Street, just to the south of the recreation ground.

5. Turn right along the High Street and make your way back towards the fine Malpas cross. You will pass the United Reform Church

to your right, and the Old School House dating from 1745 to your left. Glance along the B5069 off to the left, just opposite the fire station, and you will see some fine old almshouses. Further along the High Street to the left, just before the car park, lies a book-makers with a fine collection of horse brasses on display in the window. On your right lies the Secret Garden Craft Shop.

6. On the junction with Well Street, leading off to the left to No Man's Heath, having passed Country Pine and the bus stop, you will find the very fine Village Hall, also known as the Guild Hall, dating from the Victorian Jubilee of 1877. Now is the time to decide which of the watering houses should be favoured with your appearance.

19. Nantwich

Access

Nantwich (SJ655525) has a good network of local bus services and can be accessed by bus from Chester and Newcastle under Lyme. The railway station is served by regular services to Manchester, Crewe, Shrewsbury, Hereford and Cardiff. Nantwich can be reached by car using several A-roads. If arriving by car for this walk, park up The Gullet by the church.

Fine façades in Nantwich (Abigail Bristow)

The Town

Nantwich is a town based on a legacy of salt mining like other towns in this part of Cheshire. The town was partly destroyed in 1583 by a serious fire. It was also the site of a battle resulting in a victory for Parliament in the civil war. Nowadays a peaceful town with interesting shops, many impressive buildings and an imposing church.

Refreshments

As would be expected of a town the size of Nantwich there are numerous pubs and cafes throughout the town centre, some of which are mentioned in the text.

Nearby Places of Interest

Shropshire Union Canal

The Shropshire Union Canal lies to the west of Nantwich, this walk takes you as far as Nantwich aqueduct, but on another occasion you may wish to venture further down the towpath.

The Walk

This walk includes Nantwich Marina, if you want a shorter walk, cut out point (3) and instead turn right at the bridge and go straight to point (4).

1. The walk commences at the car park in the Gullet. If approaching from the Railway Station, go up Station Road and Patchetts Row and up The Gullet to the church.
From the car park, follow the signs for Tourist Information, past the Bowling Green Pub and then turn left down the path which takes you round the church; note the Old Wyche Theatre on the right. The Tourist Information Office is located in the Square, which also houses the War Memorial.

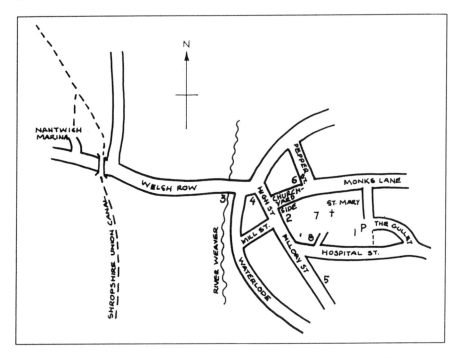

2. Turn left into the High Street and right at Ye Olde Vaults down Mill Street, cross the road and turn right down the river bank. Note the large granite boulder, originating in Dumfries and landing in Cheshire during the last ice age. The river bank also houses a plaque commemorating the great fire of Nantwich in 1583.

3. Turn left across the bridge and follow the road towards Nantwich Marina. Pass by the Cheshire Cat, now a pub, but formerly an Alms House for widows, converted from cottages in 1676. This building has extremely strange and uneven lines, looking slightly twisted. Note the mounting steps for horse riders built alongside it at the front. Walk on, past an old savings bank on the left dating from 1846. The Police Station on the right, was for sale when we walked past, obviously surplus to requirements. Continue on past the Welsh Row Methodist church. A building resembling a chapel on the right, but was actually an old grammar school, now accommodates among others the Rural Development Commission. Walking on, pass under Nantwich Aqueduct, then turn right walking through the car park into the Marina: have a look around and wander down the towpath. Note that part of the canal-side is private – this is clearly marked. Turn back and walk back to the bridge in Nantwich.

4. Cross the bridge and follow the road straight on, on reaching the Oat Market, follow it to the right. There are some very weird looking buildings along here, extremely old and fragile looking half-timbering, topping modern high street name shops, look out especially for the buildings housing the Halifax Building Society, Stead and Simpson and the Crown Hotel. The Crown was destroyed in the great fire of 1583 but was rebuilt very rapidly and acted as a stop on the London – Chester coaching run.

5. Continue down Pillory Street until you reach the Nantwich Museum housed in the old Nantwich Free Library erected by public subscription in 1889. The opening hours are Monday to Saturday 10.30 to 16.30 (closed winter Mondays). Adjacent to the Museum is the Victoria Cocoa House built to encourage temperance. Retrace your steps up Pillory Street.

6. Turn right into Churchyard Side. Have a quick look down Pepper Street, especially at the bewilderingly large range of pies offered by H. Clewlow, butchers, when did you last see a steak pie with oyster sauce?

7. Returning to the Square housing the church, which acted as a graveyard until 1854, take the chance to have a look round the Parish Church of St Mary founded in the 13th century. This church contains ancient and modern, reflecting the continuing life of the church and town, from medieval pulpit to a tapestry curtain commemorating the silver jubilee of Queen Elizabeth the Second, and a stained glass window remembering a local farmer who died in 1981. This church is worth more than a passing glance, and guides are available for purchase, near the entrance.

8. On leaving the church follow the cobbled lane directly ahead past the Lamb Hotel, then turn left, past Sweet Briar Hall, a survivor of the 1583 fire and back to the Gullet. Or cut through past the Methodist Central church to the car park.

20. Neston

Access

Neston is a small town situated on the Wirral, in west Cheshire, 11 miles north-west of Chester. Parking is available near the Railway Station off Ladies Walk at SJ292778.

The town is served by bus services to and from Birkenhead, Chester, Ellesmere Port, Hooton, Liverpool and West Kirby. Trains run to and from Bidston, where there are connections for Birkenhead and Liverpool, and Wrexham. Full details are obtainable from Cheshire Bus: phone numbers listed in the introduction

The Town

After the decline of the port of Chester, caused by the silting of the River Dee, the port was moved downstream to Neston; at the beginning of the nineteenth century, this village had the largest population of any settlement in the Wirral. By this time, however, the port had already moved downstream again to Parkgate, for which Neston was the market town and coaching station. By 1831 the main traffic had moved downstream again to Holyhead and Liverpool. Also in 1831, the population of Birkenhead began to exceed that of the now declining Neston.

In about 1761 Neston was the birthplace of a labourer's daughter who gained fame and fortune with her physical beauty. She became Lady Emma Hamilton when she married Sir William Hamilton, the British Ambassador in Naples, in 1791. Famous as Lord Nelson's mistress (she gave birth to his daughter in 1801), she was widowed in 1803 and died in poverty in 1815.

Refreshments

The walk takes you past three public houses – The Brown Horse on High Street, the Greenland Fishery Hotel on Parkgate Road (which serves meals) and the Coach and Horses on High Street. Luigi's Food and Wine bar is on Parkgate Road.

Nearby Places of Interest

Botanic Gardens

The Ness Botanic Gardens are situated one and a half miles southeast of Neston.

The churchyard at Neston (Tom Hornby)

The Walk

1. The walk starts from High Street at its junction with The Cross at SJ292775. The route leads downhill the short distance into Parkgate Road. Before setting off, note the brick building marked "WTM 1724" on the corner of High Street to the left of The Cross. This, and other early eighteenth century houses on the route, remain from the period of Neston's greatest prosperity when it was the Market Town and coaching station associated with the

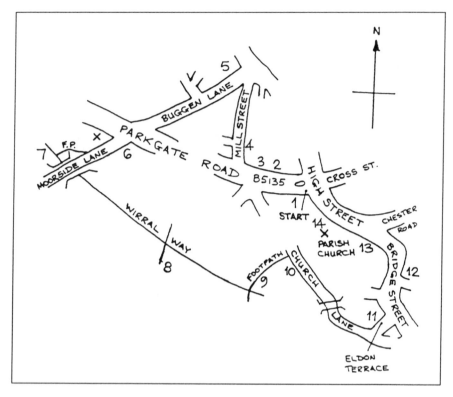

Irish traffic from the Port. Across High Street, facing The Cross, is The Brown Horse public house. In the centre of The Cross is a drinking fountain, now blocked up, erected by the townspeople for "their neighbour Christopher Bushell Esq in 1882."

2. Proceed down Parkgate Road. On the right is a decorative terra- cotta tower, a local landmark, now housing Tower Health Foods. To the left is the Greenland Fishery Hotel which sports handsome signs featuring a clipper ship. Some windows are etched, show- ing the Smoke Room and the Tap Room. Food is served in this impressive building.

3. A little further along on your right, opposite the end of Church Lane, is Vine House, a very handsome early eighteenth century building with a sundial between the windows of the upper storey. Just beyond Church Lane is the Neston Free Library and next to it is a Fragrance Garden, a pleasant spot to sit.

4. Turn right up Mill Street, a pretty street. Note, particularly, the pink sandstone terrace to the right. At the top of the street is Leighton Road with the green to the right. Across the road to the right is a building marked "ITL 1724," note again the date of Neston's greatest prosperity.

5. Turn sharp-left into Buggen Lane which leads downhill between high sandstone walls. The old wall has been breached in many places to provide access for new housing. The houses are in various styles, mostly recent. Overhanging trees make this a pleasant walk, although care is needed as there is no pavement.

6. Reaching Parkgate Road again, across the road to your left is another early fine eighteenth century building, Moorside House. Cross Parkgate Road to Moorside Lane. The United Reform church stands to the right. Note the postbox marked VR set into the wall on the left corner. Continue along Moorside Lane.

7. After a short distance, before the road reaches the bridge seen ahead, take the path to your right which leads down, past trees, to the Wirral Country Park. On joining The Wirral Way, turn left under the old railway bridge, noticing the stone abutments and brick arch typical of this type of bridge. You are now walking on the route of the railway which once linked Hooton to West Kirby. This is now a shady woodland walk. Continue until you reach a path crossing the Wirral Way. Divert momentarily onto the path leading to the right.

8. In the fence now to your left is incised "The Old Quay" – the confusing name for Neston's New Quay, which was built by Public Subscription in the 18th century. It became the Old Quay when Parkgate got the New Quay, which of course in turn became the Old Quay! From the top of this path there is a view to the Welsh Hills across the Dee Estuary. Return to the Wirral Way and continue in the same direction as before, looking out for shrews and other native wildlife.

9. Soon another path crosses. Turn left here, immediately before the gate for 'Wirral Country Park'. Follow a rough track past a white-washed wall, turning right into a metalled lane after 40 yards.

10. You are now on Church Lane. Follow it downhill between trees. The lane twists right then left as it passes under a little stone railway bridge with a low arch. It then widens out into a suburban vista, though there are some older buildings, which predominate as you continue.

11. Turn left along Eldon Terrace, built in 1885, where the original decorative brick can still be seen on the few unrendered buildings. At the end of Eldon Terrace turn left into Burton Road, noticing a nice old sandstone terrace to the right. Burton Road leads you between the abutments of a now vanished railway bridge and into Bridge Street. There are great contrasts between the building styles to be seen as the road winds into the town.

12. Pass Steeple Court. To the right is a green area with benches. Continuing, the Coach and Horses Inn is to your right. This is a very large pub, still with separate rooms and with a beer garden to the rear. Notice the interesting windows engraved "The Birkenhead Brewery Co's Celebrated Ales."

13. Beyond the Coach and Horses you return to the main shopping area of the town. To your left is the Parish Church of St Mary and St Helen. The square tower is of interest. It was built in the fourteenth century, re-using Norman masonry, and the top storey added in the nineteenth century. This was probably in 1874-5 when the church was rebuilt in its mediaeval style with the varied stone heads by the windows, and gargoyles. A plaque in the tower reads "The bells of this tower rehung in the year of our lord 1697." It is a shame that the stained glass windows of this attractive building must be shielded with hideous mesh and that it is usually locked. If you can get inside it is of interest, housing, for instance, fragments of pre-Norman crosses.

14. Circling the church clockwise you pass round the tower and then ahead will see a little sandstone building with arched doors. Pass through the iron gate beside this odd building and follow the pathway to return to High Street. Here turn left to return to your starting point.

21. Parkgate

Access

The village of Parkgate is in West Wirral, 12 miles north-west of Chester. Parking is available off School Lane at SJ278783. Bus services run to and from Birkenhead, Chester, Heswall and West Kirby. Alight at Mostyn Square. Full details are obtainable from Cheshire Bus: phone numbers listed in the introduction.

Refreshments

Parkgate is well provided with refreshment facilities. The Red Lion Inn, serves hand pulled beer and food. The Ship Hotel has bars and restaurant. Meals are available from Sizzlers Restaurant, the Copper Grill and Mr Chows Eating House. In addition, there are ice cream parlours, a sandwich bar and a fish and chip shop.

The Village

The name of Parkgate comes from Neston Park, an area enclosed in 1250 as a deer park, which it remained for 350 years. The village was not established till 1720.

In the eighteenth century, Parkgate became the principal port for traffic to and from Ireland and its quay is presumed lodged somewhere in the middle of The Parade. By 1830 the Dee had silted too much at this point to allow the bigger ships to sail and the passenger traffic moved to Holyhead and Liverpool. Parkgate, however, remained as a fashionable bathing place, The Parade being its promenade. Sea bathing had just started to be recommended as a healthy pastime.

The village still has much of the character of a seaside resort, but silting of the Dee has continued and, since the 1930s, the view from its promenade, instead of waves, has become a sea of marshy grass. The Dee can just be seen as a bright line between the grass and the Welsh hills.

The sands here, Gayton Sands, belong to the RSPB and attract many bird-watchers, especially in winter. They host shorebirds such as Knot and Dunlin as well as ducks, and birds of prey – peregrine, merlin and hen harrier are all regularly seen here in the winter months. Gayton Sands are particularly noted for a winter flock of black tailed godwit which can be identified by their cry of "Reeka Reeka Reeka!".

The Parade, Parkgate

Nearby Places of Interest

Botanic Gardens

Ness Botanic Gardens are two and a half miles south-east of Neston.

Wirral Country Park

The Wirral Country Park follows the route of the old railway which used to link Hooton with Neston, Parkgate and West Kirby. It runs inland of the village, parallel with The Parade.

The Walk

1. Start from The Parade, at its junction with The Square, otherwise known as Mostyn Square. Enter The Square with Sizzlers Restaurant to your left as you approach the church of St Thomas's. Continue ahead into School Lane, passing to the left of the little sandstone church, built in 1843 as a Congregational chapel. It has lancet windows, a bell over the door and pleasant gardens.

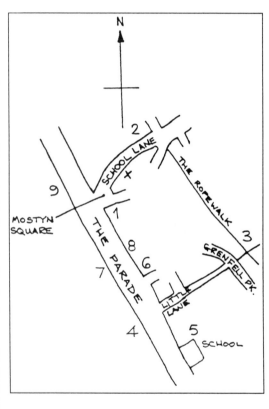

2. Continue along School Lane. To your right is the Old School House, with its bell tower and pointed windows, now a private home. At the top of the lane cross the road and take the path signed 'The Ropewalk'. This was originally used as an alternative to the seafront when the weather was bad, although the origin of the name is not known. There may be a link with the rope makers who were known in the area. The path leads between hedges, through a pleasant residential area, passing the recreation ground to your left and then a grassy area with benches.

3. After passing this field you reach a place where another path crosses at right angles. Here turn right onto this wide intersecting path. A little further on, cross a new residential road and continue along the wide, unmade, path with the school playing field to your left. A short distance further on, look to your right along Sand Heyes to a row of pretty sandstone cottages. On your right, just before you reach The Parade, notice Marine Villa with its decorative mouldings.

4. The Parade was the promenade of seaside Parkgate. Here seventeenth to nineteenth century houses and cottages (many remodelled in the black and white style) look out over the marshes of the Dee estuary. In many ways this is very much more interesting than the sea. Where else can you stand in a busy street and look out over sudden wilderness where little rodents scuttle and heron and other marsh birds fly? To your left is Nichols Famous Ice Cream Parlour. This block, also containing the Post Office, was featured as an important example of modern architecture in The Architectural Review of 1935.

5. Further to your left is The Ship Hotel and further south again is the vast bulk of Mostyn House School, once an Inn but much altered and extended. The Inn was the birthplace of Sir William Grenfell (1865 – 1940). He became a medical missionary and is remembered for his work in Labrador. There, he set up hospitals, schools and orphanages.

6. Turn right along The Parade, passing the Parkgate Ice Cream Shop and the Copper Grill. Beyond this, Balcony House sports a cast iron balcony, steps up to front doors and still retains its bell pull. The raised doors indicate how, once, the waters of the Dee Estuary could wash over the Parade. Now only the most extreme tides approach Parkgate.

7. Continue along The Parade, noticing the sea wall constructed of pink sandstone. Periodically, steps cut into the stone lead down into the marsh. It is not advisable to venture onto these treacherous marshes. On a clear day, the remains of Flint Castle may be discerned to the south-west, across the estuary.

8. To your right you will find the Red Lion Inn, formerly a trading house. It was built in about 1710 and features authentic beams. The Inn has several cosy rooms and a traditional atmosphere.

9. A little further along The Parade, you return to The Square and the beginning of the walk. If you choose to continue along The Parade, you will find a shop selling seafood. Shrimps, once a local speciality, are now imported. Here also is Mr Chows Chinese Eating House. In the distance looms the black and white bulk of the Boat House Hotel and, beyond that is a route into the Wirral Country Park.

22. Prestbury

Access

Prestbury is well served by train (daily but far less frequent on a Sunday) from Stockport, Macclesfield and Congleton. There is a bus on Mondays to Saturdays from Macclesfield.

Those travelling by car should follow the A523 to or from Macclesfield and take the A538 turning for Prestbury as signposted. From Wilmslow take the A538 to Prestbury. There is a large, free car park in the village.

The Village

Prestbury is mainly one long main street which leads from the roundabout in the village up to the railway station. It is one of the prettiest settlements in this part of Cheshire and reckoned to be exceedingly affluent by all accounts. Like many small Cheshire townships, Prestbury grew up at a crossroads and fording point of the River Bollin. It evidently enjoyed a twice yearly market where animals were bartered and a general "free for all" took place much to the consternation of the residents.

There are cottages near to the Bollin and there are several walks opened up through the Bollin Valley project which makes the village a good centre for rambles.

Refreshments

There are several restaurants in Prestbury, two cafes, and pubs, all of which you pass in the main street.

The National Westminster Bank, Prestbury (Nina Mensch)

Nearby Places of Interest

Adlington Hall

Two miles along the A523 road beyond Prestbury is the village of Adlington (which also has a rail station) where you will find Adlington Hall. Home to the Leghs of Adlington since 1315 this ancient hall dates partly from Elizabethan and partly from Georgian times. It is a mix of homely half-timbered architecture and an impressive frontage where the neo classical work is very dominant. The hall is open to the public at certain times.

Hare Hill

This Victorian woodland garden with ponds and a walled garden is managed by the National Trust. It is known for its azaleas and rhododendrons.

The Walk

1. From Prestbury railway station, a fine building which has recently been restored, turn left into the main street and walk downhill towards the centre of the village. On the right you will see the Admiral Rodney public house, a listed building of character. The front door is actually to the rear of the pub now for the hostelry pre dates the main road.

2. Go left along Bridge Green but soon after the public conveniences on the right go right along a path between houses. This right of way runs behind several dwellings and exits by a stile and gate. Go right and wander through the meadows of the Bollin Valley for no more than 200 metres before cutting right to the bridge across the Bollin.

3. This brings you to the village again at Shirley's Drive. Go left to the main Macclesfield Road. Go right and at the roundabout right again. There are several fine buildings here including the Legh Arms on the left, a Grade II listed building which used to be called

the Saracen's Head and since 1719 has been known also as the Black Boy.

4. On the right stands Prestbury church, of 13th century origin but much restored by the famous church architect Gilbert Scott in the 1870s. To the rear of the churchyard is a simple Norman chapel from the 12th century and most probably on the site of a Saxon church for there is also the remains of a preaching cross dating from pre Norman times. Across the road is a half-timbered building which was once a vicarage and is now a bank: it is known as the Priest's House.

5. The road bends over a bridge by the Bridge Hotel and across the Bollin. Retrace your steps back to the railway station.

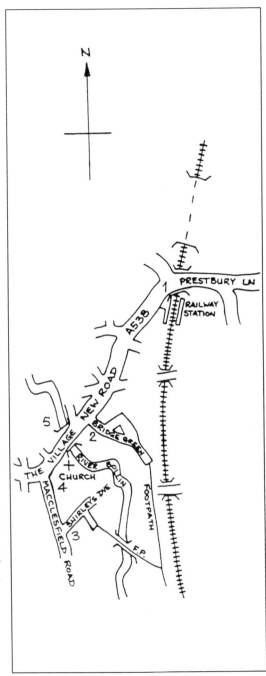

23. Sandbach

Access

Sandbach (SJ757609) lies in south-east Cheshire, one mile west of Junction 17 of the M6. The town is at the intersection of the A533 and the A534, five miles south-east of Middlewich, and six miles west of Congleton. Parking is possible in Congleton off the Congleton Road in front of the library.

Sandbach station actually lies at Elworth, one mile to the west of the town centre on the Middlewich Road. Trains serve Sandbach from Stockport, Manchester, Wilmslow and Crewe; service details on 0161 832 8353. Bus services link Sandbach with Congleton and Macclesfield and many other local destinations; for full bus details, contact Cheshire Busline on 01270 505350.

Saxon crosses, Sandbach (Norman James)

The Town

Sandbach is a fine old market town with a cobbled square. It was originally a Saxon village in the ancient Kingdom of Mercia, and was valued at four shillings in the Domesday Book. Its inhabitants were converted to Christianity in the 7th century by four itinerant priests, Cedda, Adda, Betti and Diuma, who travelled the country in the manner of the Apostles, preaching wherever they arrived. The fine Saxon Crosses on the cobbled village square were originally erected to commemorate this event in 653 AD.

Sandbach, with its market day on Thursday, well rewards some time spent wandering its streets to discover its fine buildings and monuments. There is a true sense of history to the town, and this is reinforced by its fine array of traditional shops, some of the most interesting of which are featured in our town trail below.

Refreshments

There are several fine pubs, inns and restaurants within the historic heart of Sandbach, and these are described within the text.

Nearby Places of Interest

Trent and Mersey Canal

There are many fine towpath walks along the Trent and Mersey Canal, which can be accessed close to Elworth, where Sandbach station lies, some one mile west of the town centre.

Jodrell Bank

Jodrell Bank, the famous radio telescope site and the associated arboretum, lies some six miles to the north of Sandbach and is open throughout the year. Goostrey rail station lies about one and a half miles from Jodrell Bank, and there is a pleasant country walk from the station to the radio telescope site. Goostrey station is two stops to the north of Sandbach station.

The Walk

1. The town trail starts at the village square (SJ759608), a beautiful
    cobbled medieval square, dominated by the fine Saxon crosses,
    and ringed by several interesting businesses and a multitude of

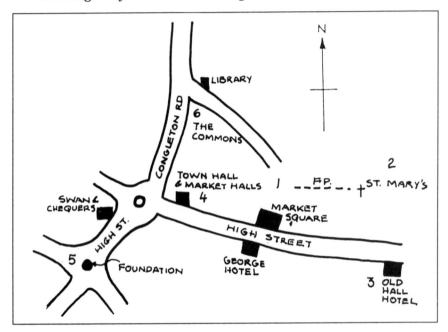

public houses. As mentioned above the crosses were erected to
commemorate the conversion of Mercia to Christianity in AD
635. The larger of the two crosses shows scenes from the Bible,
including John the Baptist in the wilderness, and various stages
in the life of Jesus: His birth, His Trial, His crucifixion and His
Ascension to heaven. The smaller cross shows events leading up
to the conversion of Peada, son of the King of Mercia to Christianity, and his eventual marriage to Alchfleda, daughter of the
King of Northumbria, Oswy. The latter would only allow this
union if Peada embraced the faith.

Take a while to explore this wonderful square, and note in
particular, in a clockwise direction: Ye Old Black Bear Inn, a fine

old inn dating from 1634 with a thatched roof and where bear baiting originally took place; the Casa Vecchia restaurant; the Market Tavern public house, which was originally used by traders to conduct their business over a pint of ale; the Crown public house, which serves a fine pint of Robinsons, which still retains its essential character, and probably dates from around 1680; the Lower Chequer Inn claims to be the oldest building in Sandbach, dating from 1570 – note the mounting block at the side allowing travellers to mount and dismount into and from carriages and horses; Godfrey C Williams and Sons, a fine old traditional speciality grocers and delicatessen, dating from 1875 and housed in what was originally a police house. Most of the other shops and businesses around this delightful square also inhabit attractive and historic buildings.

2. A pathway to the side of the grocers will lead you to the church of St Mary's: the churchyard contains many fine mature trees affords fine views of Sandbach High Street and beyond. The present building was erected in 1661, and was encased in new stone around 1850. It is likely that there was a timber and thatch church on site, together with a priest at the time of the Domesday book. It is possible that a stone church has stood here since around AD 1200. The roofs of the nave and side aisles are carved out of fine Cheshire oak, and were manufactured for the original church opening in 1661.

3. Walk down from the church to the High Street, and admire the fine black and white building which is the Old Hall Hotel, probably dating from 1656. The Hall was originally the residence of the Lords of the Manor of Sandbach. Turn back along High Street towards the village square, and you will come to Hopkins Gunmakers to your left; just beyond, and opposite the Square, lies the George Hotel, one of Sandbach's original coaching inns, and well over 300 years old. The George boasts a bowling green, a resident ghost, a fine collection of brasses and oak beams. The London stage called every day at 4.00 pm; other stages called en route to and from Liverpool and Birmingham.

4.   Walk further along High Street, and you will soon see the fine Town Hall, with the Market Halls behind, to your right, which displays its table of tolls on the wall, and has a good selection of fine old shops in its foyer. The Town Hall was constructed by local builder, John Stringer, in 1890. The market moved from the square to its current site in 1879, when Lord Crewe gave Sandbach the perpetual right to all tolls from the market, plus the site for the new Town Hall: a market has been held in Sandbach since 1579.

5.   From the Town Hall turn left at the roundabout into High Town: note the fine building housing the Swan and Chequers public house, built in 1895. It is believed to be the only pub of this name in the country, and may originally have been a corn market. The fountain in the centre island was a gift again from Lord Crewe, and was erected in 1895, and is resplendent with palms. The Sandbach Literary Institute to the right was built in 1857, costing £2,500, and was constructed in the Gothic style. Ramsay Mac-Donald once addressed a meeting here. The adjacent Trustees Savings Bank was built in similar Gothic style in 1854 by Thomas Stringer.

6.   Return now to the Town Hall and walk along Congleton Road, passing the market halls and the market site on Scotch Common:. these Commons got their name from the battle that took place there in 1651, when a troop of Scots retreating after the Battle of Worcester rested on this open space land, but were set upon by local Sandbach folk attending the Thursday market: many were killed and the rest taken prisoner and kept in the church. If you take the road to the left of the Commons past the new library, you will soon be able to turn up right along a path which will lead you back onto the Square arriving between the Market Tavern and the Crown. Now you have to decide where to refuel yourself and reflect on this historic and unique south Cheshire market town.

24. Siddington

Access

There is only a very limited bus service from Congleton and Macclesfield to Siddington on Saturdays (Bus 75) but it is feasible to have an enjoyable trip given the bus timings. Those travelling by car should head for the A34 road between Broken Cross and Congleton. Turn down Fanshawe Lane (near the old school) for parking.

The Village

Siddington (SJ846708) is a very traditional village which is still associated with agricultural ways of life. There is no shop or pub here but you will find the loveliest of churches in these parts and a

The church at Siddington
(Norman James)

gathering of folk on most days at the water's edge of Redesmere. The church looks to be of half -timbered construction but a closer inspection reveals that this is merely exterior dressing. The curiosity is, however, that the brick walls conceal the 14th century timber framed construction. The spring is the best time to visit as the daffodils are out and the pretty little bell turret adds so much to the character of this place of worship. It was evidently an addition to warn parishioners of a possible invasion by the Spanish Armada. History did not unfold this way and the bells peeled a victory celebration instead.

A mile up the road is Capesthorne Hall, the home of the Bromley-Davenport family since the Domesday Book. The Hall, with its amazingly long facade, dates from the 1730s mainly but also contains alterations from the 1830s and, after a disastrous fire, restorations from the 1860s. It has many fascinating period rooms on display which are open to the public. The gardens and parkland are equally impressive, especially the three linked lakes near to the hall.

Nearby Places of Interest

Jodrell Bank

No one can miss the enormous radio telescopes of Jodrell Bank. The complex is open as a science centre and there is also a superb planetarium. Not so well known is the arboretum with dozens of rare trees to observe.

Swettenham

About three miles from Siddington is the out-of-the-way village of Swettenham, which is well known for its daffodils in spring. Daffodil Dell is found near to the mill and the ford which leads up to the church and the Swettenham Arms. It makes for a lovely stroll, especially when combined with a visit to Siddington.

The Walk

1.   Start in Redesmere Lane. Facing the waters of Redesmere go right.

This is one of the many natural meres in the area resulting from glacial activity. The mere is home to a variety of wildfowl which love to be fed by those who come for an afternoon stroll and ice-cream here. It is also a water which attracts sailing and fishing too.

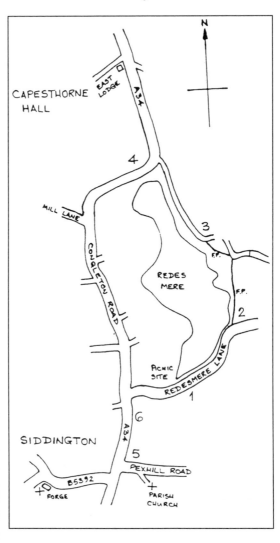

2. As the lane bends left and then right go left over a stile, the path is signposted to Capesthorne. It is well worn and easy to follow. Cross two fields and stiles then bear left through woodland.

3. At the gate you join a track. Go right to follow the track through a pasture up to the main road. The views back across the mere are excellent. Once on the pavement you have a choice. You can either go right if you intend to visit Capesthorne. The lodge gate is not far. Cross over the road to enter the Capesthorne grounds but check with the hall beforehand to ensure that it is open.

4. Otherwise go left. You will have to cross to the pavement on the opposite side of the road. This is a good path for it leaves the edge of the road, which can get busy. This passes a craft workshop, the old school and Redesmere Lane before it reaches a staggered cross-roads. Go right into the village to see the forge and a cluster of old cottages up to the junction.

5. Walk back to the staggered crossroads and cross over Pexhill Road to visit the church. There is a restored cross in the church-yard and an ancient yew. The gravestones provide a veritable social history of the village. Inside, the church is simple and the timber work is to be admired. Situated near to the church is a workshop for the making of 'corn dollies' – an ancient English craft. There is a small museum, often open to visitors.

6. Return to the main road, go right and right again back to Redes-mere Lane. Those travelling by bus will be set down and picked up near to the church by the crossroads.

25. Styal

Access

S tyal is served by train from Manchester and Wilmslow on Mondays to Saturdays, but the service is fairly limited. There is a bus service from Wilmslow. Car drivers should use the B5166 from Wilmslow. There is limited parking in the village and parking for visitors at Quarry Bank Mill.

Styal village (Chris Rushton)

The Village

Styal village stands back apace from modern society which almost encroaches it year on year. It is a living example of an industrial village designed with purpose on humanitarian as well as commercial lines. Most of the neat rows of red-brick terraced houses were built in the 1820s to house the expanding work-force at Quarry Bank Mill. It was built by Samuel Greg in 1784 and was in use until the last days of 1959. It is now a beautifully restored working museum reflecting the earlier stages of development in the cotton industry in the north-west of England. It is managed by a mill trust for the National Trust.

The Apprentice House, built in 1796, was home to large numbers of boys and girls drawn from workhouses and orphanages by Greg to work the looms. By our standards life was tough but the small school and Norcliffe Chapel provided education and spiritual guidance for the young workers. Moreover, they escaped starvation. The House illustrates life here in 1830, a welcome contrast to much of the squalor and hapless existence of many proletarian families working in other mills.

Refreshments

There is a shop and the Ship Inn in the village as well as a cafe at Quarry Bank Mill.

Nearby Places of Interest

Styal Country Park

The 274 acre park allows you to explore the beautiful wooded Bollin Valley. There are several way-marked walks. The area is the subject of concern as the proposal for a second runway at nearby Manchester Airport might have a detrimental impact on the locality.

The Walk

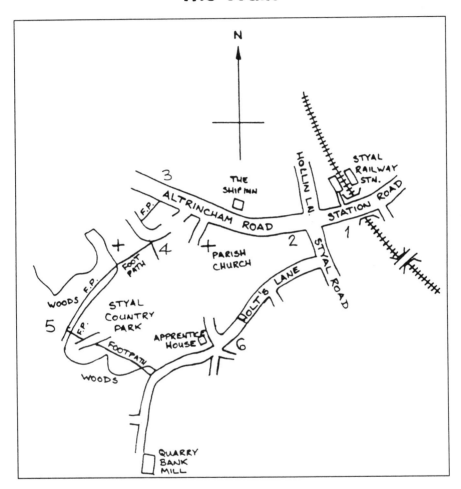

1. Leave Styal Railway station to walk down Station Road to the junction with Hollin Lane.

2. Go right and then turn first left into Altrincham Road. On the right is the Ship Inn and on the left a post office and stores. Walk down the road until you reach the National Trust car park on the left. You will pass by a sign for Norcliffe Chapel but do not go this way.

3.   Go left as signposted to Styal Village by Oak Cottages. After the National Trust Estate office, go next left to walk to the village cross which is reckoned to be of medieval origin. Before you do, look right to the window display of the co-op store. You will also be impressed by the cultivated cottage gardens and the neatness of the village green. It really is a model village to this day.

4.   Turn right for Norcliffe Chapel and Styal Country Park. Visit the chapel and then proceed on the same path into the woods. The path forks and you keep left through a mature section of mixed woodlands.

5.   Pass by the footbridge on the right, built as part of the centenary celebrations, and cut next left to leave the wood. This brings you to a track near to the Apprentice House and the drive down to Quarry Bank Mill. You can see and hear the machines humming, weavers at work and all manner of activity. The massive driving water wheel is an attraction on its own. The exhibits and working demonstrations make this an exceptional place to visit. It is a must. Retrace your steps back to the Apprentice House.

6.   Go ahead here to cross an unmade track and walk up Holt's Lane to Hollins Lane. Return to the railway station.

26. Tarporley

Access

Tarporley (SJ553625) lies 12 miles east of Chester, just south-east of the junction between the A49 and A51. A public car park is signed off the high street behind the Rising Sun pub. The car park is divided into two sections, the part closest to the pub is the Rising Sun car park, this will be chained off out of hours, so ensure that you park in the rear public car park.

The Village

Tarporley is a typical Cheshire linear village – there are many fine Georgian facades to admire around the village centre.

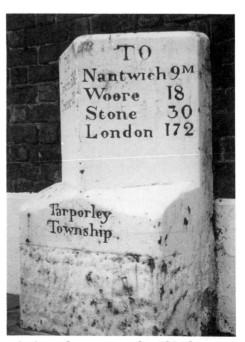

Refreshments

There are several pubs and hotels in Tarporley, offering food and drink: these are mentioned within the text. There are also a few tea shops, but note that these are closed on Sundays.

Ancient milestone, Tarporley (Abigail Bristow)

Nearby Places of Interest

Oulton Park

For fans of motor racing Oulton Park circuit lies a few miles east of Tarporley.

Sandstone Trail & Shropshire Union Canal

Those seeking a more pastoral pursuit might investigate the Sandstone Trail to the west, or the Shropshire Union canal to the south.

The Walk

1. The starting point for the walk is the Rising Sun; with your back to the pub, turn right along the High Street. Notice Market Court off to the right containing the Old Smithy. Continue past the Swan Hotel, and what was once a fire station and is now "The Old Fire Station Chocolate Shop" – a curious change of use.

2. Note the best kept village award for 1992 and head down the narrow Church Walk to your right, past small shops including a little tea shop and into the churchyard.

3. St Helen's church is constructed of red Cheshire sandstone, there is a war memorial to the front, commemorating the dead of two world wars. To the rear of the church is an old school house dated 1626. The graveyard is itself attractively laid out and well cared for – remember to abide by the prominently displayed graveyard rules – the Done family are well represented. There are very attractive views across country and a footpath to Birch Heath. Emerge through the lychgate and recommence the walk along the High Street, past the Manor House, dated 1585, with attractive work around the window sills.

    Views open out as you approach the Tarporley Antique Centre, a collection of small antique shops located in one building and well worth a look. The road now takes you past the Crown Hotel

(Burtonwood beers) and Tarporley Baptist and Methodist church, dating from 1866, but with an unusual modern glass frontage.

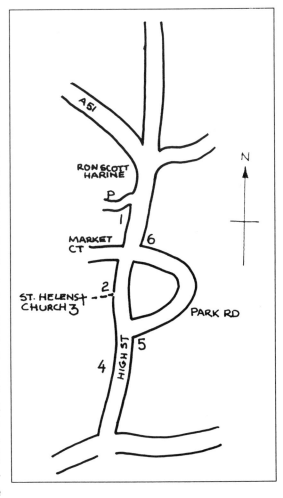

4. Turn back up the High Street at the Forresters Arms, a local Greenalls pub with pool table in the tap room. Cross the road to proceed along the other side, past a tiny pet shop.

5. Turn right up Park Road and you will see a compact fire station to the left, with appropriately red doors: these can only conceal a small fire appliance! Continue past a school and a slightly incongruous telephone exchange, follow the road round to the left. Off to the right lies a stile and footpath signed across the fields to Cobblers Cross. Walk on past the hospital and the road bears left again, past a joinery with rocking horses, model planes and other interesting toys on display. The road now emerges back into the High Street.

6. Turn right into the High Street and on past Lyns Larder (a tea shop), on past Tarporley Fish and Chip Shop to a road signed to Ukinton; it is worth following this road for a few hundred yards as it climbs above the surrounding countryside to offer splendid

views across Cheshire. Return to the High Street and walk back down it. At Ron Scott Marine, a footpath is marked, again it is worth following this down to the first stile, for the views across to what appear to be a castle and of the resident squirrels; this path forms part of the Sandstone Trail.

Return to the road, past the Number six coffee shop and back to the Rising Sun. It's probably time now for some refreshment, in a local pub or coffee shop.

27. Tarvin

Access

Tarvin is in west Cheshire, five miles to the east of Chester, near the junction of the A51 and the A54. On-street car parking is available. It is recommended that you park to the south of the village centre in Church Street, beyond the church at SJ492669.

Bus services run to and from Chester, Northwich, Nantwich and Crewe. Alight near the church where the walk begins. Full details are obtainable from Cheshire Bus: phone numbers are listed in the introduction.

Church Street, Tarvin (Tom Hornby)

The Village

Tarvin (SJ492670) is a small village, its centre built on an outcrop of sandstone rock. This old settlement is named from the Welsh word Terfyn, meaning boundary, and it features in the Domesday survey as one of the larger Cheshire manors.

In the Middle Ages it was on the edge of Delamere Forest, which was then much more extensive than now. Mediaeval forests were used for Royal hunting and other uses were restricted, so that, even today, there are no towns and few sizeable villages in the area. Delamere was only officially deforested in 1812.

By the fourteenth century the church of Tarvin was the centre of a large Parish and Tarvin had a market in Tudor and Stuart times. In the eighteenth century, however, a fire destroyed much of old Tarvin and it was reconstructed as an eighteenth century village. The market was discontinued. A mediaeval souling play was performed on All Souls Eve (31st October) until the 1920s, but little remains of the culture of old Tarvin now except the ringing of the Pancake Bell each Shrove Tuesday.

In the 1770s the London road was re-routed through Tarvin but more recently by-passes have been created to carry traffic round the village and it is now a quiet spot.

Refreshments

There are two pubs: the George and Dragon and the Red Lion. Both serve food. Tarvin also has a chip shop.

Nearby Places of Interest

Hockenhull Platts

A mile or so south-west of the village are the three little bridges known as Hockenhull Platts. These, at one time, carried the main London road over the River Gowy and are well worth a visit. Strong shoes are advised if making this trip.

The Headless Woman

The name of the Headless Woman public house at Duddon is said to originate from the fate of Grace Trigg, a servant at Hockenhull Hall who was beheaded by Cromwellian troops during the Civil War. Hockenhull Hall is now occupied by the British United Turkey Company.

Delamere Forest

Delamere Forest lies five miles north-west of Tarvin on the B5152. Most of this is now Forestry Commission owned and a forest trail runs from near Delamere village. Here bird-watchers will find many visiting species in summer including warblers, cuckoo, redstart and tree pipit; sparrow hawk, woodpecker, goldcrest, redpoll, siskin and crossbill can be seen at all times of year.

The Walk

1. The walk starts from the church in Church Street (SJ492669). Enter the church grounds, admiring the distinctive gravestone to the left which bears three heads, and circle the church with its handsome gargoyles. Building was commenced in the fourteenth century. Of particular note is the single framed, arch braced roof of the south aisle, the oldest surviving timber roof in Cheshire. The stained glass was removed and the sculptured images defaced by John Bruen, the squire of Stapleford and an ardent Puritan. The building is usually locked but a notice on the door informs you where you can borrow the key. From the rear of the pleasant grounds can be found views across the nearby fields. Note the well kept brick built farmhouse and outbuildings visible from the rear of the church, typical of many to be seen in Cheshire.

2. Leave the church, noticing on the right the remains of the early grammar school founded in 1600. This school was one of several founded at the same time as a number of the Oxford and Cambridge colleges during a period when literacy and education were of increasing importance.

3. Turn right towards the centre of the village. Continue the short distance northwards to the junction of the old main roads at the centre of the village. Here stand the two village pubs, both of which were coaching inns. To your left is the Red Lion, a modest sized building which has been altered internally, having only one bar, but with a friendly atmosphere. The George and Dragon is larger and has a very pleasant lounge bar as well as a separate local's bar. To your right will be found a fish restaurant.

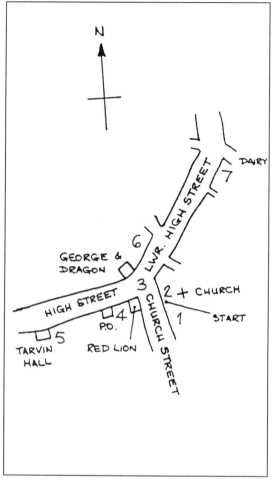

4. Take the left turn at the junction into High Street. The width of the street is a reminder that Tarvin once had a market. Here, to your left, are the general store, Post Office and newsagents. A leisurely stroll westwards reveals several items of architectural interest. Note that many houses, particularly those to you right, are founded directly onto the sandstone bluff. Several buildings seem to have been rebuilt onto the foundations of earlier structures. A timber framed cottage can be seen to your right, opposite Bull Cottage. Unfortunately, at the time of our visit, this was in a poor state of repair.

5. Continue the short distance to Tarvin Hall on the left at the top of the brow. Here a Dr Brindley ran a boarding school for boys in the nineteenth century. Observe the odd circular windows set into the stone wall of this building. Now retrace your steps to the George and Dragon and bear left into Lower High Street.

6. A short walk along Lower High Street reveals a more mixed character. Some buildings here are quite modern while others are extremely old. Note the house on the right next to the Zion Primitive Methodist Chapel, with its foundation cut into the sandstone rock, and be sure to explore the fascinating lane to your right between 76 and 82 High Street; the construction of the old houses here is particularly interesting.

7. You now reach the entrance to the creamery on the right. Northern Dairies has its regional headquarters in Tarvin and is the principal employer in the village. From here return to the centre of the village and your starting point, possibly pausing for refreshment at one of the hostelries previously mentioned.

28. Tattenhall

Access

Tattenhall (SJ488585) lies in south-west Cheshire, one mile east of the A41, at a point two miles north of its intersection with the A534 Wrexham to Nantwich Road. Parking is mainly on-street in Tattenhall, except for patrons of the various public houses, and it is recommended that parking is done to the east of the village centre on the road to Newton.

Tattenhall is served by bus services to and from Chester, Malpas and Whitchurch. Full details are available from Cheshire Bus (phone numbers are listed in the Introduction).

The Letters Inn, Tattenhall (Norman James)

The Village

Tattenhall is an attractive linear village on the edge of the Cheshire Plain surrounded by some attractive hills. The mountains of North Wales are evident to the west. Red Cheshire sandstone is often to be seen here, both in situ and pressed into use as a building material.

The main street is lined by good timber framed cottages and Georgian brick terraces: there are many outstanding cottage rows and impressive town houses.

Refreshments

There are three major public houses in Tattenhall, which in addition to real ale, offer a warm welcome, home cooking, and the chance for a cup of coffee. Full details are contained within the text.

Nearby Places of Interest

Cheshire Farms Dairy Shop

The Cheshire Farms dairy shop at Newton offers freshly made ice cream.

Cheshire Candle Workshop

The Cheshire Candle Workshop lies three miles from Tattenhall.

Beeston Castle

Beeston Castle, three miles from Tattenhall, is an English Heritage property, and open for viewing throughout the year (see also Beeston).

Footpath

The attractive public footpath to Burwardsley, access from SJ491584, lies to the east of the village.

The Walk

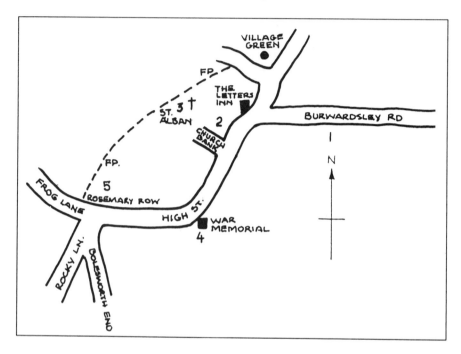

1. Starting from the eastern edge of Tattenhall (SJ491584), the route takes you north-west along the High Street with attractive cottages to either side. Vernon's Butchers Shop, a fine old-fashioned traditional shop can be seen on your left, just before the Sportsman's Arms Public House.

2. Further along on the right lies The Letters Inn, where a fine pint of real ale and an extensive menu can be enjoyed, both in the bar and the adjoining dining room. There is often a fine open fire. Opposite the Letters Inn lies a particularly fine row of cottages. Turning to the right just before the Letters, brings you to the Village Green and Primary School. We will, however, continue our way along the High Street, passing the Bear and Ragged Staff Public Houses on the left. Opposite this hostelry is a private house with a notice warning potential visitors that the dog of the house "takes no prisoners!"

3. Just beyond Gosmore and Sons, another traditional family butchers, lies Church Bank on the right, which will lead you to the attractive church of St Alban, fashioned out of red Cheshire sandstone. The churchyard is peaceful and attractive. Note the lovely little cottages along Church Bank, and in particular the black and white gabled National Westminster bank. Retrace your steps to the High Street and admire the fine town houses opposite: Orchard House, set back from the High Street; The Mount, a beautiful black and white house with veranda to match; and Rock Cottage, dating from 1601.

4. A short distance further along on the left lies the pleasant and moving War Memorial, just beyond the fine building of the Balfour Institute, dating from 1897; quite often there are a couple of Shetland ponies grazing in the field behind. Pass over the Golthorne Brook and the road bears to the right past the Tattenhall Centre, for educational activities.

5. Just past the attractive black and white Beehive Stores on the right and the road junction on the left, take the footpath on the right. Pause to admire Rosemary Row Cottages and Rose Corner opposite: these splendid estate cottages were designed by Clough Williams Ellis of Portmeirion fame to resemble a Palladian manor house, replete with portico. Follow the footpath back to the village green, crossing back over the Golthorne Brook, and taking time out to admire the views of St Alban to the right, and the fine old Brook Hall to the left.

Having arrived back at the start of the walk, your key decisions are which of the fine hostelries to visit for refreshments, and which of the nearby sites and attractions to visit to round off your stay in south-west Cheshire.

29. Wilmslow

Access

Wilmslow is well served by trains from Stockport and Crewe. There are also several bus services from local towns, including Macclesfield and Knutsford, arriving in Bank Square. There is easy road access from the M56 along the A538 and from both north and south along the 'old' A34 (C466 from Alderley Edge, C467 from Handforth). The 'new' A34 now by-passes Wilmslow. There is car parking near to the Leisure Centre and by the Carrs recreation area, which is on this walk.

The Town

For many the Wilmslow of old has gone. Such landmarks as the police station in Bank Square, the Rex cinema and many small shops have given way to supermarkets and wine bars. This may well be the case but there is one enduring feature, the Bollin Valley, which has for decades provided recreation for the dwellers of Wilmslow. It forms the core of this town walk.

Wilmslow is said to have gained its name from 'Wilghelm's Mound' referring to an early Saxon stronghold. The church of St Bartholomew stands at the centre of the old quarter. It has an interesting churchyard as there are many well preserved tombstones dating from the 17th century. Up-river towards Prestbury is the site of an old silk mill (later, a calico mill) which burnt down in 1923. The riverside meadows known as The Carrs stretch down the valley towards Quarry Bank Mill at Styal – the path is known locally as the Apprentices' Walk, this being their route to church on the Sabbath.

Wilmslow Parish Church (Chris Rushton)

Refreshments

There are several cafes, restaurants and several pubs in Wilmslow so refreshment will always be nearby.

Nearby Places of Interest

Alderley Edge

While the town itself is pleasant, most visitors head for the Edge where there are dozens of woodland walks from the National Trust car park (near The Wizard restaurant) along the Edge. The area is rich in folklore and legend as well as being riddled with caves and minor underground excavations which can still explored under the guidance of the local caving club.

The Walk

1. From Wilmslow railway station, turn right into Station Road. Cross the A538 (old A34) into Swan Street and then Bank Square; several buildings around here, including the police station in nearby Green Lane, are Victorian. The wine bar at the corner of Swan Street and Church Street was the Union Bank, after which Bank Square is named.

2. Turn right into Church Street. After passing the George and Dragon, you come to the church of St Bartholomew's – Wilmslow's parish church. If it is open, step inside to view the fine interior including several 17th century tombstones and the oak roof of the chancel. A small 14th century crypt has been turned into a beautiful small chapel.
    Opposite the church is a memorial garden for those who lost their lives in the two world wars of the 20th century.

3. Continue down Church Street into Chancel Lane. Go left to enter The Carrs by a children's playground. Keep on the path near to the riverside until you reach Pownall Bridge (toilets here). This

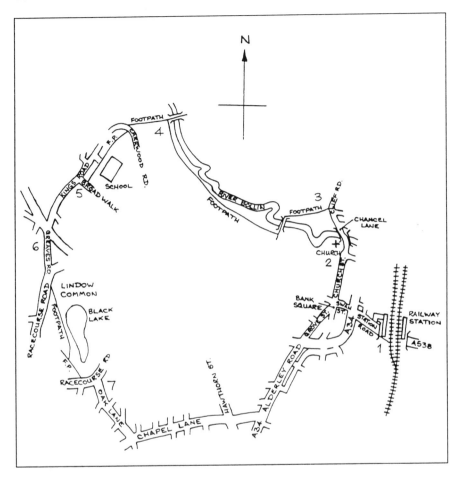

was on the route followed by the Styal Mill apprentices to the parish church. Do not cross the bridge, but turn left and walk up the rough track by the rugby club to the bottom of Carrwood Road.

4. Go left into Carrwood Road and then first right up a narrow signposted path before the first house on the right. This runs between houses, gardens and Pownall Hall school. It passes Pownall Farm (no longer a farm) to exit onto Broadwalk.

5. Go right and then first left into Kings Road. This soon comes to the main Altrincham Road (A538). Cross over to an unmade road which runs to the rear of the Boddington Arms.

6. This takes you to Racecourse Road. Cross the road to Lindow Common and then keep on a path to the right of the small pool. Lindow Common is part of the much larger Lindow Moss, which is still used as a source of peat for agricultural purposes. It was also the scene of a major discovery in 1984. Lindow Man, dating from the Iron Age, was excavated here after being preserved in the peat for centuries. By all accounts he met with a gruesome death and this has been the source of many a news item since. The path continues to Black Lake – a popular angling and dog-walking route. Do not walk around the lake, instead turn right (keeping the lake on your left) and then straight ahead to Racecourse Road. Leave the common through a stile and cross Racecourse Road into Oak Lane.

7. Follow Oak Lane to the crossroads at Chapel Lane. Turn left here. Pass by shops and one of Wilmslow's more traditional public houses, The Farmers Arms, on the right. Continue, pass the Carter's Arms on your left and go over a crossroads to continue to Alderley Road. Turn left here and walk back through the town centre and along Grove Street, which is now pedestrianised, to Bank Square. Pass the Swan Inn on your right.

8. Cross the A538 (old A34) towards the railway station. The large pub opposite, called The Rectory, really was the 18th century rectory for Wilmslow, even though it is a fair distance from the parish church. Prior to being a pub it was unoccupied for many years before being acquired by the National Westminster Bank, who refurbished it.

The area between The Rectory and Wilmslow town centre is Parsonage Green, where Rector Thomas Wright fought off a Roundhead attack. This is one of several "greens" in the area – others are Lacey Green and Davenport Green.

Note: if you arrived by bus, you should start and finish the walk in Bank Square.

30. Wybunbury

Access

Wybunbury is an attractive linear village, in the shape of a semi circle, lying in south-west Cheshire, three miles east of Nantwich, four miles south of Crewe on the B5071 just north of the A51. Car parking is available on-street throughout the village; it is recommended that you park on-street at the south side of the village beyond the church tower and cemetery at SJ700498.

Bus services run to and from Crewe and Nantwich. Full details are obtainable from Cheshire Bus: phone numbers are listed in the Introduction.

The Village

Wybunbury is named after Wyburn, King of Mercia, who died in 615 AD. An interesting feature of Wybunbury is the old church tower, which is all that now remains of the old church, rebuilt in 1892, but subsequently collapsed. The tower acts as a fascinating landmark for the village, and it can be very pleasant to sit in the grounds surrounding it.

Refreshments

Food and drink are available in both the Swan Public House and the Red Lion Inne. The Swan has a garden to the side and rear and particularly fine views into the surrounding countryside.

Nearby Places of Interest

Footpaths to Hough

The various footpaths leading from the old church tower to Hough offer enjoyable jaunts.

Bridgemere Wildlife Park

Bridgemere Wildlife Park lies three miles south of Wybunbury on the A51.

Wybunbury Moss

Wybunbury Moss can be visited if special permission is obtained from the Warden; He can be contacted on 01565 830226, and can advise you when the next guided tour will take place. Please note that it is dangerous, and a trespass, to visit the Moss without permission.

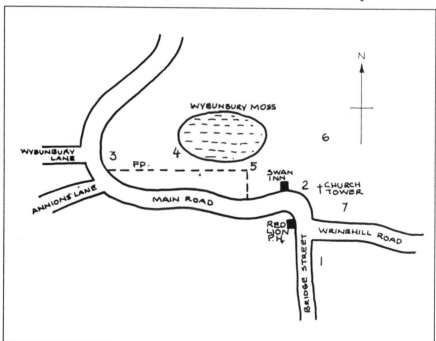

The Walk

1. The walk starts from the "overflow" cemetery at the southern edge of the village (SJ700498). Walk northwards, past the road junction to the right, and turn up the pathway towards the old church tower. It is very pleasant to wander in these grounds and to enjoy the fine views afforded of the surrounding countryside. Note that many of the flags used for the paths are tombstones.

2. Pass around the old tower and exit the grounds by the Swan Inn. There is a fine view of the Moss from the pub car park which also houses an antique shop. The Swan Inn is an attractive old pub with several bars and lounges. Almost opposite lies the Red Lion Inne, a red brick building with a locals' bar and a smart lounge. Continue your way northwards along the Main Street, unless you are already tempted by these fine hostelries. Fine cottages, mainly of red brick line both sides of the Main Street. Pass by the Methodist church to your right, and the attractive, quaint General Stores and Post Office to your left. An attractive ivy covered cottage lies to the right of the Street, and the new Village Hall and the pleasant Grannies Cottage lie to your left. Behind this latter cottage lies the recreation grounds. Bear right round the bend with the road, passing the new church to your left.

3. Just before a junction to the left, take the well-marked footpath to your right, which will lead you back to the village centre by way of Wybunbury Moss. Pass over the field along this footpath which is generally kind on your feet. Pass over the first three stiles, and you will come upon Wybunbury Moss to your left.

4. Wybunbury Moss, managed by English Nature, lies in the wooded hollow to your left. It is both an interesting and dangerous bog, home to unusual plant and animal life, such as bog rosemary, sundew and the green hairstreak butterfly. A species of spider previously unknown to Britain has recently been discovered by scientists in Wybunbury Moss, which is believed to date from the Ice Age. The black spider, known as Gnaphosa Nigerrima, and reaching eight millimetres in width, is found on the continent of Europe and is believed to have become isolated in Britain when the island broke away from the rest of Europe some 7,000 years ago. A whole population of such spiders has been found in this quivering moss: this makes a total of 240 species of spider in the United Kingdom. The Moss consists of a raft of peat, only one metre thick in places, floating on a water-filled depression which may be up to 12 metres deep. It is believed that this water-filled cavity was formed by the solution and erosion of salt-bearing rocks. Do not enter the Moss without permission: this would be both foolish and illegal. The site manager can be phoned on 01565 830226, and will be pleased to give details of the next guided tour of the Moss. Particularly fine views of the wooded canopy of the Moss can be obtained from your footpath as you follow it in a straight line over a succession of five further stiles. (Note that at one point it is necessary to skirt around a foliated roundel in a private driveway in order to resume the footpath).

5. After the final stile, turn right and return to the main street. If you fail to turn right, the geese which are normally in the field ahead will warn of the unwary traveller's approach. You can now return to the old church tower and explore the various footpaths.

6. To the north the footpath leads over the fields to Cockshades Farm, affording pleasant views including the Moss.

7. If you take the path to the east, the footpath initially leads you down a flight of steps set out of tombstones. Turn right along the track and right again to lead you back to the beginning of the walk. Alternatively, turn left on the track, pass immediately over a stream, and pass over a stile on the footpath to Hough. You will pass close by the remains of an ancient moat to your right.

Index

Other titles of interest from:

TEA SHOP WALKS IN CHESHIRE

Join Clive Price on his mouthwatering tour of Cheshire. Splendid country walks all with the tempting promise of an authentic Cheshire afternoon tea as your reward!

£6.95

CHESHIRE WALKS WITH CHILDREN

This book from **Nick Lambert** was the first in our "Walks with Children" series and it has quickly become a firm favourite. Things to look out for and questions to answer along the way make it an entertaining read for young and old alike.   *£7.95*

PEAK DISTRICT MEMORIES: the photographs of E. Hector Kyme

Roger Redfern

E. Hector Kyme (1906-1987) was a renowned photographer whose work appeared in a wide range of publications. His great love was the countryside, high hills and farming life. He knew the Peak District intimately, from a lifetime of cycling and walking there. Roger Redfern, a long time friend of the photographer, has selected a representative sample of photographs taken over the last thirty years of Hector Kyme's life to form this fascinating view of the Peak District National Park and adjacent fringes. Superb photographs and entertaining text make this truly a collector's item.

£9.95

For further details of these and many more fine books, please contact:

Sigma Leisure, 1 South Oak Lane, Wilmslow, Cheshire SK9 6AR
Phone: 01625-531035; Fax: 01625-536800; E-mail: sigma.press@zetnet.co.uk

Free catalogue. ACCESS and VISA orders welcome – 24 hour Answerphone service! Most orders are despatched on the day we receive your order – you could be enjoying our books in just a couple of days. Please add £2 p&p to all orders.